Daddy Smarts

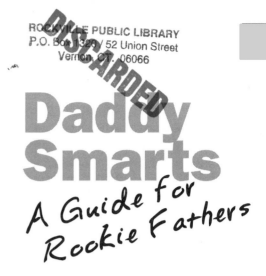

Daddy Smarts

A Guide for Rookie Fathers

Bradley G. Richardson

Taylor Trade Publishing
Dallas, Texas

Designed by Barbara Werden

Published by Taylor Publishing Company
1550 West Mockingbird Lane
Dallas, Texas 75235
www.taylorpub.com

Library of Congress Cataloging-in-Publication Data
Richardson, Bradley G.
  Daddy smarts : a guide for rookie fathers / by
Bradley G. Richardson.
      p.   cm.
  Includes index.
  ISBN 0-87833-164-6
  1. Fatherhood. 2. Fathers—Life skills guides.
3. Pregnancy—Popular works. 4. Childbirth—
Popular works. 5. Father and infant. I. Title.
HQ756 .R5 2000
306.874'2—dc21   99-056764

10   9   8   7   6   5   4   3   2   1

Printed in the United States of America

This book is dedicated to the most
important people in my life—
Meredith, Samantha, and
Skylar Richardson

my True Companion
my "Sam-a-lama-ding-dong"
my "Mr. Man"

Thanks for making me a Daddy.
It's a job I'm proud of.

A hundred years from now it will not matter what sort of house I lived in, or what kind of car I drove, or what my bank balance was, but the world may be different because I was important in the life of a child.

ANONYMOUS

Contents

Part 6 Life A.B.—After Baby

Acknowledgments

Talk about right place, right time! If you don't believe in divine intervention, serendipity, or just dumb luck, let me tell you how I came to write this book.

I've written several successful business books, but after the birth of my daughter three years ago I wanted to share what I was learning about being a father. Initially, the idea fell upon deaf ears, so I shelved it and went back to business topics. But after my son was born, I became reenergized and decided to pursue my goal with a new passion.

Last fall, on a flight from New York home to Dallas, I noticed that the woman next to me was reading book proposals. Being in the book business myself, I struck up a conversation and found that she was, indeed, an editor. We talked shop for a while and learned that we had much in common and were at similar stages in our lives. I decided to ask her opinion on my idea for a kind of "Guy's Guide" to pregnancy. By the time we landed three hours later, we had decided to pursue it. The rest is *Daddy Smarts* history.

So first and foremost I want to thank that woman on the plane, Camille Cline. She is someone with whom I see eye-to-eye, both editorially and professionally; a pleasure to work with and infinitely patient. Thanks, Camille, for believing in this project and in me.

I also want to thank Fred Francis, who was a huge help in editing the manuscript, and the rest of the Taylor staff. Thanks also to Pam Bernstein and Donna Downing. And thanks to the many parents I spoke with who were kind enough to share their stories, thoughts, joys, and fears. I couldn't have done it without them.

Many thanks to the friends and family who have been so supportive throughout my career by helping me turn an idea into reality. I'd like to thank my friends Steve and Shana Javery for being there for me throughout all my books, and especially Steve for his support and many trips to Starbucks when the girls were pregnant. Thanks to my brothers-in-law Tate Smith, James Introligator, and Craig Introligator.

Thanks also to my in-laws, Jack and Jan Introligator. You're awesome grandparents and I couldn't have asked for a better family. Jack, thanks for being such a great role model. A huge thanks to my sister Paige Smith, who helps me stay on the right track, have faith in myself, and keep my head screwed on straight. You know me so well. I can't thank my biggest fan, Judy Richardson, enough for being mother, father, friend, and counselor, and for teaching me how to be a loving parent. I'm forever grateful. You've done a good job and I love you.

Most of all I want to thank the most important people in my life: my wife Meredith and my children Samantha and Skylar. They are the people for whom I get up in the morning and who make life worth living. Thank you for your love, your understanding, your patience, your faith in me, and most of all for being my family. Meredith, you are my true companion. I love you.

Bradley G. Richardson
Dallas, Texas
March 2000

Introduction

Every nine seconds a baby is born in the United States, and in that split second that one life begins, countless others are changed forever. Each year over four million American men share that singular life-changing experience of becoming fathers.

Actually, their lives began to change about nine months before that magic moment, when they first learned their wives were pregnant when they began "negotiating" with their spouses about whether or not even to have children. Man and woman working as a team toward the common goal of creating a healthy little life ... it sure sounds great. Unfortunately, that goal is about all men will have in common with their wives throughout the next nine months.

Becoming a father is one of the most wonderful, enlightening, crazy, scary, frustrating, and enjoyable experiences a man will ever go through. Yet, traditionally, the focus throughout pregnancy, childbirth, and even child rearing has been on women.

And hey, why not? After all, they do much (okay, most) of the work but often overlooked are the ones who help make all of this possible: men.

Prospective dads have no shops, no showers, no special parking spots, no special wardrobe options (unless you count shorts and dark socks), and few books ... until now. Simply look around the mall, the grocery store, or your local bookstore to see how everything focuses on, supports, cherishes, educates, and exalts mothers.

Hey, What About Me?

I asked a simple question during my wife's pregnancy: "HEY, WHAT ABOUT ME?"

I realize that this doesn't portray me as the enlightened sensitive man I should be. But neither am I a Cro-Magnon who expects my wife to be forever barefoot, pregnant, and making me a turkey pot pie. I prefer to think of myself as a cross between James Bond and John Gray. You know, the Marlboro Man who can cry ... but doesn't.

The point is that fatherhood is a life-changing event and while men aren't the ones giving birth (thank God), they go through many changes emotionally and face concerns that, while dramatically different, are as real and important as those of mothers.

There are over seventy million twenty- and thirty-somethings in the United States. While men of all ages become fathers, this age group is the most active (unless you count Anthony Quinn, age 85). This group, who were the first generation of latchkey kids, that is, those whose mothers regularly worked outside the home, are coming of age and beginning to have children of their own. And believe me, attitudes and expectations about being a parent are very different from those of our fathers.

Ward Cleaver? Forget About It

Today about the only place you will find Ward Cleaver, or any father like him, is on Nick at Nite. The days of men waiting outside the delivery room and passing out cigars are long gone. Childbirth, and child rearing for that matter, have become a team effort, with much of the emotional and physical workload—as much as is physically possible, at least—being shared.

My sixty-something father-in-law, who has never changed a diaper and never will, views his lack of domesticity as a badge of honor. I, however, father of two small knee-biters, am well versed in the ways of poop. Fatherhood has changed.

Today, 53 percent of all new moms work. Employed married fathers spend more time with their kids than such fathers did twenty years ago. There is no road map for parenting, and our fathers couldn't prepare us for what men face today. A recent study by the Families and Work Institute claims that there are increased parenthood pressures in two-income families over those in which one parent stays at home.

Dad Is Job One

Men today want to have a greater role in their children's lives. Studies have shown that kids tend to veer off track and get into trouble without the proper influence of a dad. We are now seeing the fallout of a divorced, stepfamily, dysfunctional, workaholic lifestyle. Many men want to truly experience fatherhood, and women want and need them to be active participants in the parenting process. Visit a day care center anywhere in America; close to half the parents dropping off or picking up kids are men. Go to a play group at your local Gymboree, Discover Zone, or Little Gym any Saturday morning, and you will find that fathers make up almost half the class.

Even companies are buying into it. Marriott has recently developed courses on fathering skills for their employees. And last year, in a bold move that shows how the role of fathers has changed, FBI director

Louis Freeh, top lawman in the United States, took three months of paternity leave, taking advantage of the Family Medical Leave Act, stating that he wanted to spend time with his wife and new son.

Where Do Guys Turn?

As a prospective dad, I wanted to be an active participant in the pregnancy, yet I found little information that was geared for men.

My search of Barnes & Noble and Borders bookstores around the country yielded little. I searched Books in Print and located only five books whose main subject entries listed fathers and pregnancy. All were obscure books written either by a woman, a Ph.D., or a comedian. All were either more technical than I needed or wanted or were mushy tomes on the virtues of fatherhood. I ended up reading my wife's books. Like many women who learn they are pregnant, she had immediately trucked off to the bookstore to spend a couple of hundred dollars on every pregnancy book there was.

I learned a lot, but there were certain concerns, fears, and questions I had that were very different from anything my wife was going through. In looking at the guides for women, I found the whole forty-week, blow-by-blow description thing annoying. Sure, women are going through these changes daily, so they need to know every little detail. But for a guy, how different is week twenty-six from week twenty-seven?

The one that did it for me was Vickie Iovine's *The Girlfriends' Guide to Pregnancy*. Your wife probably already has it, and if not, you should buy it for her. It sounded like women who get together with their friends and talk about what they are going through, offering advice, thoughts, fears, and lessons learned. It certainly helped me learn more about my wife. Yet it still didn't help me, the average (okay, slightly above average) male, with what I was going through as a future father.

Like you, I am an intelligent man who was seeking knowledge and answers. A man who desperately wanted to gain control mentally of what was going on around him. It's not like I was some oversensitive wuss who decided to acquiesce to everything my wife said for nine months (as some books suggested). Nor did I subscribe to the Tim Allen *muy machismo* mind-set. I was a romantic; I got engaged on top of the Empire State Building, for God's sake.

When my buddies (those who were in similar predicaments) and I would go out for our sanity-saving "Guy's Nites" (video games and too much Starbucks), we discussed the matter. We determined that we guys didn't need a clinical analysis of what was going on with the fetus and our wife's body. Nor did we need a satirical view of what for us were real issues. Ditto for smarmy tales of the joys of fatherhood. We wanted the real scoop. Will I be a good father? Will I be like my father, and is that good or bad? How will we pay for this thing? How will I care for a baby? Why can't we get pregnant? I'm not ready. My wife's not ready. How will I juggle career and family? Will I ever have sex again? When do I get my wife back? How will this change our marriage? Will I pass out or throw up at the delivery? She doesn't want to go back to work, but we can't afford it. What did I do wrong? How do I baby-proof the house?

Unfortunately, until now the market for fathers was largely underserved. Still, it's not like you see guys hovering around the pregnancy and parenting sections of your local bookstore, unless they are accompanied by women who are (or at least hope to be) carrying their seed. C'mon, admit it—chances are pretty good that you received this book as a gift. Fortunately, realizing that you would probably read this just to humor your wife, I decided to take advantage of the situation and write something that guys might actually like. Before we get started, though, let me give you a brief primer on what was previously available to dads and how it has affected what you will and will not see in this book.

An Assumption

As I pointed out previously, some fathering books treated me not only as though I were uninformed (which I was), but as though I were just stupid. I'm going to assume that you are a reasonably intelligent man who is competent in his personal and professional life. When it comes to fatherhood and pregnancy, however, it is okay to be uninformed. Don't worry if you don't know it all, or even if you don't know anything. After all, you're a rookie and all dads have been there. That is what this book is for, to help you learn from other dads' experiences. Some of the topics may seem basic, but my promise to you is this: I will treat you like a rookie, but I will never treat you like an idiot.

One More Assumption

Every book for expectant fathers I've read makes it a point to overemphasize a woman's sensitivity to the size of her rear end. I vow to break the cycle. This must stop. I'm going to assume that you were smart enough and sharp enough to get this woman to marry you and eventually sleep with you and bear your child. That alone takes some smarts. However, if you are the type of man who seriously needs to be reminded that it is not only bad form and rude but downright stupid to comment on the size of your wife's butt, then you need more help than this or any other book can provide and probably have no business reproducing. Please put this book down and schedule a vasectomy right now.

Super-Celebrity Dad Profiles

There are dad books by celebrities that chronicle their own experience and those of other celebrities such as hockey legend Wayne Gretsky. Now I love gossip, biographies, and tabloids;

I even read *People* magazine (my wife subscribes). But let me tell you, as a regular guy with a working wife and a mortgage, I don't know if Wayne Gretsky and I have that much in common. For some reason, I really don't think "The Great One" is at the Babies R Us checkout line thinking, "I can't believe how expensive formula is."

Ughh—Me Likes Pictures

When I first discovered pregnancy and fatherhood books, their approach made me wonder whether men are expected to actually understand words on a page. The overabundance of smarmy cartoons and drawings I saw didn't tell me what I needed to know. The authors seemed to feel that men can't comprehend fatherhood without pictures to aid them.

TMI: Too Much Information

I'm not a doctor and I don't play one on TV. I chose another profession, because I abhor blood, guts, and bodily functions. As an expecting father, I will not be taking the medical boards at the end of nine months, nor, I hope, be called on to actually deliver the baby. I trust the doctor and his or her training and expertise; this will not be a medical textbook.

I also believe in a person's right to privacy. There are some things I don't want to know about my wife and her insides. Call me old-fashioned, but I want to save a little of the magic and mystery behind the female form. For these reasons, I will not go deeply into female anatomy and physiology.

If you require this, please check out your wife's books. *What to Expect When You're Expecting* is a great one for in-depth technical information regarding women's bodies.

Who Are the Players?

What qualifies me to write this book? I'm thirty-three and have been married for five years. My wife and I both work full-time. In addition to being an author, I run a human resources consulting firm in Dallas, Texas, and my wife is a professional and full-time working mom as well.

My wife also happens to be extremely "hot," I might add. This is important for you to know because in about eight months, after your wife has gained forty pounds, you will be wondering if she will ever return to her previously "hot" status. I'm here to tell you, have faith, brother, she will.

We have two adorable kids: a four-year-old girl, Samantha, and a two-year old boy, Skylar. I'm what they call a veteran Daddy—I've fought the wars and lived to talk. And it's not like I'm telling you what it was like to be a daddy twenty-five years ago. I'm living it as we speak, in the ultimate OJT—On-the-Job Training. I'm also not a multigazillionaire who could genetically engineer my kids and have them available only for photo ops with my supermodel wife. I'm an active daddy twenty-four hours a day, seven days a week.

My research includes my own experience and that of other daddies

I've spoken with from around the country. I'm here to tell you that the *Daddy Smarts* presented here are 100 percent road tested by real dads. This is active fathering. This is the straight scoop. The smart stuff. So if you want the poop (a word you will become familiar with soon enough) on becoming a father, then turn the page and get ready to become *Daddy Smart*.

PART 1

Life B.C.— Before Conception

Life seems wonderfully uncompli-cated before you learn that you are to become a father. In just a few months, you will never look at your life the same way again.

Please fasten your seat belt and keep your hands inside the vehicle at all times ... it's a wild ride.

1

The Negotiation

We had only been married a little over a year when we first had "the talk." It was early on a Sunday afternoon and we had just left the house of friends who had given birth to a baby girl two weeks before. The reason for our visit was to attend a baby-naming ceremony (similar to a christening).

Beautiful young couples filled the room. Unfortunately the room was divided much like a junior high school dance: women on one side, cooing and oohing over the beautiful little baby, and men on the other, their hands sheepishly in their pockets, making conversation about anything other than kids. Well-intentioned but obnoxious older folks only added fuel to the fire by asking younger couples, "So, when are *you* two going to have children?" Most guys wanted to respond, "When donkeys fly, now leave me alone, you old bag," but instead smiled politely and said, "We'll see."

This couple was the first in our group of friends to have a child, so every guy in the room knew what was in store for the ride home. He could look forward to being pressured and hot-boxed into starting a family ASAP.

My wife Meredith and I left the party and decided to go house hunting, as we like to do on Sundays. We weren't buying, just wishing and looking at the big dream houses we hoped to buy when we started our family. As we pulled up to a beautiful home, which was well beyond our budget, I turned to Meredith and noticed that she was on the verge of tears. Thinking I must have committed some faux pas back at the ceremony, I asked, "What's wrong?"

Just When Things Are Going Well

Her bottom lip quivered slightly. "I want a baby." Being a calm, caring husband (and wanting to get out of this situation as quickly as possible), I said, "Honey, I want a baby too … someday. Now let's go see the house."

She looked at me with huge doe eyes, and her quivering lip soon gave way to full-blown sobbing. She said, "No, I want a baby *now!*" and somewhere at the back of my mind, I swear I could hear a bell: "Ding, ding!" Round one had just begun.

Not long after you marry, the pressure starts to build. Just when you have your life on track, the career is humming, and you and your spouse are finally getting used to each other and adjusting to married life, some well-meaning relative sets the wheels in motion by asking, "So, when are you two going to have children?"

More Haggling Than a Street Bazaar

If you and your spouse are at that point of deciding whether or not to have children, you may well be engaged in a full-scale negotiation. The pressure, the haggling, the emotions, and the jockeying for power can be trickier than a hostage situation.

It all begins with a little dealing, a little persuading; finding common ground, making solid arguments for your case, and trying to refute those you disagree with. Every great partnership begins with two people trying to get on the same page. Am I talking about making a contract, a treaty, a business deal? Sure sounds like it. But instead of two powerful executives or high-priced attorneys, picture husband and wife.

In the car that Sunday afternoon, when my wife hit me squarely in the face with "I want a baby *now,*" several

thoughts raced wildly through my mind. Why does it have to be now? I like our life as a couple. We can't afford a child. I'm too busy with work. I wouldn't know what to do with a baby. How can I possibly have a child when I still act like one myself?

These are the reasons that many guys balk at having a child. Following, I discuss why husbands and wives often think the way they do, and how to deal with the concerns of each.

Why It Has to Be Right Now

"My biological clock is ticking." If your wife is over thirty (and certainly if she is over thirty-five), age can be an important factor in her wanting to have a child … and quick. The risks associated with childbirth, to both mother and child, increase dramatically after age thirty-five. You may not have given much thought to how many kids you want and how old you'll be when your kids are growing up, but believe me, your wife has probably thought it out in detail.

My wife is a couple of years older than me, so even before we had our first child, she had mapped out how many children we would have, how we should spread the ages apart, and how old she would be when she had each one. We have since deviated from the plan, as most couples do once they realize the amount of work children require.

The point is, your wife may not want to be thirty-nine years old with three kids under five. She may be scared of the risks of giving birth beyond a certain age, so she wants to get started *now*. Even if you've never been around children, you can imagine that taking care of small kids requires a lot of energy, but think about carrying them in your body. Pregnancy is a strain on any woman, but even more of one the older she gets.

Another reason women want to start *now* is that they often fear having difficulty in conceiving. They are right. Many men don't realize that couples frequently have difficulty becoming pregnant. We like to think it's simple: my equipment works and so does hers, so let's do it and have a baby. But it can be, and often is, much more complicated than that. Some couples try for months or even years to conceive, and once they do (whether naturally or with fertility treatments), there is still the one-in-six risk of miscarriage. You can never be sure how long it will take to conceive. Be aware that this is a very real concern; don't dismiss the subject when your wife brings it up. The fact is, you can't take for granted that your wife will become pregnant the first time you try.

We Can't Afford It

"Let's wait until we can afford it" is the number one defense guys use when the "I want a baby" negotiations begin. Let's face it, kids aren't cheap. They are small and don't eat much at first, but they make up for it later in life. Plus, they require a lot of expensive gear. If you feel screwed when buying accessories and extras for a car, you are going to feel completely violated when it comes to buying baby stuff. Babies come into the world naked, without instructions or warranty. Everything else is extra.

You and your spouse may just be starting out. Money may be tight with only two of you, so a third may seem like a huge stretch. You may have debt to pay off before having a child so that you can start with a clean slate. You may be in an apartment and want to save for a house before having kids. You may want that fishing boat or 60-inch TV or … okay, let's not go there. You get the point. You can always find something else to spend your money on.

Be prepared for your wife to counter with wisdom handed down through the ages: "If we wait until we can afford to have a child, we'll never have one." Sorry guys—she's right. There never *is* a perfect time. "Let's wait until next year.… Let's see how this year goes.… Let's see if I get a raise.… What will we do without your income?" All are valid concerns that will keep you up late at night, but the point is that your kids (while tiring and expensive) will bring you more joy than any amount of money.

A child does bring additional expenses, but aside from day care (which is tough), the really big costs won't come until they are older. So it may be a stretch, but don't use "we can't afford it" as an excuse to postpone having kids; otherwise, you really will be too late. There will always be something else that you want or need to do with the money, so quit your whining and bite the bullet. Besides, you need to have someone who can mow the yard and take care of you when you're old and have no teeth. But be realistic about financial concerns. Don't purposely increase your responsibilities if you are barely making it now.

How Can I Have a Child When I Still Act Like One?

Besides money, responsibility is one of the greatest fears men cite when deciding whether or not to have children. Taking care of a child is a tough concept to grasp. To some men, having a kid is confirmation that you really are an adult … with real responsibilities.

Some guys view themselves as youthful, cool, and contemporary (kinda like me) and figure that being a dad doesn't fit that description. They envision a father as a balding, beer-bellied old man in coaching shorts and dark socks, driving a minivan. In fact, we picture our own fathers, who despite their best efforts to wear clothing from The Gap are never going to be cool.

Relax. You can still be cool, fun, playful, in shape, and (yes!) a stud and still be a dad. In fact, women find you more attractive if you have a child with you. Don't ask me why; all I know is, my single brother-in-law has asked to borrow my daughter to help him scope out women.

It is often hard for a man to admit immaturity or fear of responsibility to his wife. He must admit, first, that he is still a child himself; second, that he doesn't know how to take on the challenge of being totally responsible for another human being. You won't

come to terms with this one for a while. And when you do, it won't be some lightning bolt or pivotal moment. You will mature over time, rising to each occasion and gradually becoming more responsible.

Some guys view fatherhood as a loss of freedom and fun. But consider, other people already depend on you, like your wife. When you got married, you swapped one kind of fun (dangerous sports, motorcycles, wild spending, wild times, wild women) for another kind. Now you and your wife have a great time together, and you don't miss your former life at all. (Okay, maybe just a little.)

Well, having kids is also a different kind of fun. Fatherhood is not a loss of youth at all. Actually, you can live your own childhood all over again. Not only can you play with your kids, you can buy all those toys your parents wouldn't let *you* have. As a dad you can still be youthful and even childlike … just not childish.

How Many Kids Will We Have?

Unless you are on fertility drugs or multiples run in your family, most couples generally have one child at a time, not a litter. Sooner or later, though, you'll have to negotiate how many children you hope to ultimately have. Feelings regarding family size are personal and can depend on the type of family you come from.

I came from a small family, with one sibling seven years younger than me, so I wanted several kids who were fairly close together in age. My wife came from a family with three kids, all within two or three years of each other. We both love kids and decided that we wanted four kids, assuming we could afford it.

About three months after we had our first child, I was seriously re-evaluating my original desire to have four. Too much work. I wanted to scale back to three. I talked with Meredith about this when it came time for number two. She still wanted four. Not three, but four. Why? My wife read a book about birth order once that brainwashed her on the subject of birth order.

According to my wife, if you have three kids, someone is the middle child, and middle kids are either superstars or losers. So we had to have either two or four kids—but not three. I argued that if we have four, don't we get two middle kids instead of one? I also asked what happens if we have three and for some reason, we are unable to have a fourth. What do we do, tell child number three, "I'm very sorry, but you have to go back. We only have room for two on the roster"?

We went round and round about this and finally (slow-witted man that I am) I thought, why am I fighting it? Men, please: the smart thing to do in this negotiation is to simply say "okay," then worry about it later. Is this caving in? No way. Is it procrasti-nation? You bet, and it works. Here is why.

Not long after our second child was born, I came home from a business trip. Meredith had been alone with both kids for four days and looked as though a truck had hit her. She was tired and beaten. I asked how things

went and she said, "You know, I don't know about having four kids." I knew I had won. We have agreed to negoti-ate a third at a date yet to be deter-mined.

Don't worry or fight about some-thing until it happens.

We Can't Have a Baby Next Spring; How Does October Look?

If you and your wife are lucky enough to become pregnant soon after you start trying, then congratu-lations. It usually isn't that easy. How-ever, your wife may try to plan her pregnancy around seasons, holidays, or even special events. It sounds like the most anal thing in the world, but your wife may have seemingly stupid (and some not so stupid) reasons for wanting to conceive at a certain time. If timing is an issue, realize that preg-nancy actually takes ten months, not nine—forty weeks (give or take a week or two). So when you are calcu-lating around certain events, under-stand that there is no exact way to determine the due date.

However, wives will continue to plan around dates, events, and sea-sons that men would never have thought of. The wife of one veteran daddy was trying to plan for her child to be born during the school year (but not December). Her reasoning was, "I don't want my child to have a sum-mer birthday. The kids with summer birthdays always miss out because no one comes to the party. And kids who have their birthdays in December always get fewer presents because of the holidays." Do you think she might have been a bitter little summer-birthday child herself?

My wife had a legitimate reason for wanting to be pregnant when she was. She would only consider being pregnant in the winter, saying, "There is no way I will be pregnant during a Texas summer. Big *and* hot will not do." Sure enough, she was pregnant during winter.

While your wife is planning the baby calendar, you would be wise to put in your two cents' worth about when the best time would be. For example, if you are an accountant, you and your wife might want to stay away from an early April due date, if you want to be present and alert. My busiest time of the year is in the spring. I travel a great deal, speaking and consulting around the country, so I requested that we stay away from having a springtime baby. I didn't

want to deal with the guilt and stress of juggling work and family responsibilities, but sure enough, my kids were born in March and April.

As a result, I turned down a lot of business during those months around my first child's birth because I didn't know when she would arrive and my wife was convinced that I would miss it. Ultimately, I was there for my wife and family and wouldn't have traded it for anything, but I was a bundle of stress because of my work.

The point is to try and work out your schedules so you both can be there mentally, not stressing about other things. Also be flexible. Just because you want a baby in November doesn't mean it will happen. You don't just snap your fingers and become pregnant. (Okay, of course you don't become pregnant by snap-

---

It is not always guys who want to hold off or who aren't ready. Shortly after David and his wife were married, he wanted to start having a family. "We were broke and just starting out, but I really thought, 'I will get two jobs, sacrifice, do whatever it takes, but let's have a baby and everything will just work out.' His wife, on the other hand, was adamant: "We will not have a baby until we get a house. I won't have a baby while we are in an apartment."

According to David, his wife wasn't planning on having kids until they had a "nest." So they waited four years until they could afford a home. "As soon as

we bought the house, her attitude changed and she was ready to go. A week after we moved in, she would greet me at the door ready to start making babies."

If you or your spouse feel strongly about having a "nest," you both need to respect this desire, then set a time frame and dedicate yourselves to saving for a home. However, there is nothing wrong with having a child while you are living in an apartment. Whether you rent or own has nothing to do with the type of parent you will be and is no reflection on your stability.

ping your fingers, but you get my drift.)

Tell Her What You're Thinking or Fearing

Here is how *not* to handle the negotiation: blow her off, avoid it, or fail to tell her what is on your mind. As I've pointed out, much of your reluctance to discuss the baby issue may have everything to do with you and nothing to do with your wife. She doesn't know that. She may go on thinking that you just don't want to have a baby at all or that it's something to do with her. Don't be afraid of appearing weak. Talk about it with your wife and work through it.

Set a Time Frame and Stick to It

After much negotiation and discussion, you and you wife may have decided to start trying to become pregnant. If so, good luck and get busy. The next chapter is for you. But if you both have decided to wait a little bit, in other words, you have bought yourself some time, then agree to a specific time frame to either start trying or to seriously discuss it again.

After my wife and I had our "I want a baby" pow-wow in the car that Sunday, we discussed it for several more weeks and agreed to begin trying to become pregnant in six months. Sure enough, six months down the road we started trying. Set a definite time frame and be realistic. If you set a time frame and tell her that you plan to start trying in a month or a year, stick to it. Don't set a time

frame or agree to try later as a tactic to postpone or stall. That's leading her on, and can be a big problem for your marriage.

Instead, veteran daddies recommend that if you and your wife have agreed to become pregnant in six months, then buy the big screen TV in five months.

DADDYSMARTS TOP TIPS **on THE NEGOTIATION**

- **You can't take it for granted that your wife will become pregnant the first time you try.**
- **Don't use "we can't afford it" as an excuse to postpone having kids. You will always find something else that needs to be done or that you want to do with the money, so quit your whining and bite the bullet.**
- **When your wife wants to talk about having a baby, don't blow her off, avoid the subject, or fail to open up. Your reluctance may have nothing to do with your wife but she doesn't know that. She may think that you just don't want to have a baby at all or that your reluctance has something to do with her.**
- **Pregnancy lasts forty weeks (give or take a week or two). You can estimate, but there is no exact way to determine the due date.**
- **If you set a time frame and tell her that you plan to start trying in a given month or a year, stick to it. Don't set a time frame or agree to try later as a tactic for postponing or stalling.**

2

Conception

As guys, we like to think we
know everything there is
about all things sexual, but
your eighth-grade health
class and your own college exploits
have done little to prepare you for the
fine art of "making babies," as it is
technically called.

I know what you're thinking.
"C'mon man, I know this. In fact I've
been practicing for quite a while and
I'm pretty good at it. Go ahead, just
ask my wife. Or, well, on second
thought …" When it comes to actually conceiving a child, our male egos
bristle: "How hard can it be? You
have sex. Bada-bing, bada-boom.
Voila: Baby. I can do that."

Three Kinds of Sex

Sure, you have sex to make a baby.
But guys who are single or MWK
(Married Without Kids) often fail to
understand that there is sex for fun
and then there is sex for business.
Oops, that doesn't sound right. What
I mean is, there are three kinds of
married sex. First there is "pre-

fatherhood sex" and then there is
"sex after the birth of your children
when they finally sleep through the
night." Both are fun and somewhat
similar to the sex you probably knew
as a fumbling high schooler in back
seats, in basements, and on golf
courses across America, except now
you know what you're doing. Or so
your wife lets you believe.

The third type of married sex is
"sex to become pregnant." This is a
game with completely different rules.
Now, don't get me wrong. Millions of
times each year couples have sex no
differently than usual in hopes of
becoming pregnant. And sometimes
pregnancy inadvertently happens.
Many of you have probably been
called "Mother's little blessing," "our
little surprise," or some other euphe-
mism for "accident" by your parents.
If you and your wife conceive easily,
then congratulations. Keep up the
good work and have a shag on me.

However, other couples go to great
lengths to stack the biological deck in
order to produce a child. I'm not talk-

ing about surgery or drugs, although many couples must rely on them. I'm talking about putting your sex life into overdrive. It's ironic that when you were seventeen you could *look* at a girl and there was a strong possibility she would become pregnant. Now that you are trying to have a baby, it has become a systematic process with the precision timing of a Swiss watch.

I'm sure some of you reading this are anticipating the prospect of nonstop sex. "Oh yeah, I can't wait to get started and I hope it takes a long time. I could get used to this."

Well, listen up, stud. Veteran daddies say that you're right. Sex aplenty is one of the great benefits of making babies. However, they also say that you might find yourself saying there is such a thing as too much sex.

Sex to conceive is fun and exciting, or certainly should be, but some veteran daddies say you will be amazed at the clinical quality your lovemaking may take when your wife decides to actively conceive.

Honey, Can You Move a Little Bit to the Left?

Many rookie daddies ask if some positions are better than others for conceiving. Some guys don't care, they just like having a lot of sex. We all have our favorite positions, I'm sure. No need to share. However, if your goal is to conceive, some positions do work better than others.

There are entire books devoted to positions to promote conception. While the mechanics are the same for

all positions, it is widely agreed upon that the tried and true missionary position is considered the best chance for conception, although there is no hard data to back this up. Other positions thought to increase your odds are from behind or side by side, which seem to offer a better chance of sperm reaching the cervix.

Positions considered less effective include those with the wife on top or anything involving sitting, standing, or a trapeze. Seriously—gravity works against you in these positions. You want the sperm to have the best possible chance of reaching the cervix and heading up the fallopian tube.

If I can be a little graphic here—after all, this is the sex chapter—everyone's sex patterns, preferences, and habits vary. Your postcoital routine may involve getting ready for round two, rolling over and going to sleep, channel surfing for *SportsCenter,* or cuddling with your spouse in a General Foods International Coffee moment, listening to Kenny G. Regardless of your routine, your wife may discreetly go off to the bathroom to take care of some personal business and dash back in a moment.

Well, when you are trying to conceive, you can forget about your wife making that trip down the hall. In fact, you can rest assured after you've done your job, *no one is going anywhere* for about twenty or thirty minutes. Normally, if you aren't using condoms, your wife will discreetly remove your deposit from her body shortly after sex. But if you're trying to conceive, your wife will attempt to keep your semen as long as possible to give your sperm every opportunity to make the long journey to the egg.

One way women can do this is by elevating their legs. Now, you might be thinking, "If they didn't have their legs in the air in the first place, we wouldn't be in this situation." But some experts do suggest that a woman keep her pelvis elevated with a pillow placed beneath her for as long as thirty minutes to keep the sperm moving toward its intended target.

Can Different Positions Increase the Chances of Having a Boy?

No. Certain positions will not help your chances of having one sex over another. However, you can try what my buddy Scott suggests. He recommends that while having sex, just as you arrive at the critical moment, you shout "Oh, boy!" as loudly as you can. Wise man, Scott. He has two girls.

There are tons of old wives' tales about trying to alter the sex of your child. Certain gurus claim that you can influence the sex of your child by your sexual position, the foods your wife eats, which day of the week you have sex, and whether you wear boxers or briefs. There are whole books out there on this. One buddy's wife bought one. She not only read it, she lived it. She could not be talked out of it. My friend won't even tell me all of the unique rituals and idiosyncrasies involved.

There are some scientific procedures out there that have allowed a few people to choose the sex of their child, but they are experimental and there are still ethical debates going on about whether they should be made available. The bottom line is that you cannot naturally determine the sex of your child through intercourse, diet, or other special mojo.

Despite the fact that this stuff is pure bunk, if your wife believes in it, then you need to take one for the team. Just go with it no matter how senseless it may seem. She may already be nervous enough (more about nerves in a minute), and destroying her confidence or making her self-conscious is not going to help. Your job (besides the obvious) is to make your wife feel special, comfortable, confident, and relaxed.

Both of You May Be Nervous

Since high school, guys have been programmed to think of sex as recreation, not procreation. The main concerns of many young American men coming of age were (a) "How can I find someone willing to have sex with me?" and (b) "If I can find someone willing to have sex, how can I not get her pregnant?" Now that you are married and attempting to have a child, years of programming and instinctual behavior must be unlearned. This may be the first time you will have had sex with a purpose as opposd to previous experience, which can be a little disconcerting. Phillip, an attorney in San Antonio, says, "It can be a little scary because you know that you are about to have sex that can change your whole life."

Your wife may be nervous as well. Although she may not say anything to you about it, she may be wondering if she will conceive easily or not. On the other hand, most veteran daddies claim that they have found their wives to be incredibly uninhibited during this time. Think about it. You don't have to worry about contraception or getting pregnant.

"I Know Where You Two Are Going"

If you and your wife are actively trying to have a child, then you have to decide whether to share this news with others. There is no right or wrong answer to this. It is between you and your wife whether to let others know that you are mating like wild rabbits. There is something to be said for letting others know that you are ready to start a family. It is good to have a support system in place so they can express their joy when it finally happens and their concern should something not work out.

Personally, however, I'm against it. I have talked with couples at parties or dinners who annouced to everyone that they were trying to get pregnant. They would then make a production of leaving early, doing everything short of announcing on the public address system, "Attention, we are now leaving so we can go home and make hot monkey love in hopes of producing another obnoxious person like ourselves." Depending on who

the couple was, the visual usually kind of grossed me out.

If you decide to let the world know you are trying to have a baby, people will constantly ask if you are pregnant yet, make comments, and generally poke their nose in your bedroom. It might not be so bad for you, but your wife will have to deal with other women commenting on her weight, how she looks, and gossiping about "Is she or isn't she?"

Decide how you both feel about this. You and your wife need to be on the same page where this is concerned. The last thing you need is to confide in a buddy that you and your wife are trying to get pregnant, only to have your buddy tell his wife. The next thing you know, the four of you are at dinner, your friend's wife opens her big mouth, and you are getting the evil eye from your wife because you blew the secret.

During an interview for my first job out of college, I was asked by the recruiter, "If you could be any animal, what animal would you choose?" Rather than choose the brown noser, type A, overachiever answer most employers were looking for (tiger, eagle, lion), I thought for a moment and said: "That's easy. I'd be a racehorse." I'd actually been to the horse track the previous weekend and it sure beat saying "rat" or "weasel." I wasn't prepared, however, when the recruiter then asked me *why*. I fumbled around, lost in my attempt to be cute, and finally said: "They pet you, they feed you, and they put you out to stud." Not the politically correct answer most employers are looking for, perhaps.

But c'mon, isn't that the way you want to go? Sex all day, oats all night? Whoopee. But let me assure you that after talking with countless dads who have gone through assembly-line-like conception, I think they might wonder if the horse has such a good deal.

It's Still Better Than Yardwork

Don't get me wrong. Constant sex certainly beats the hell out of mowing the yard. But MWK's (Marrieds Without Kids) don't understand the clinical quality that sex can have during conception. It's not all Playboy Channel-type rendezvous. Hey, it could be … and why *shouldn't* it be, ladies? But the truth is, you will be pounced on regardless of time, place, or mood.

Jeremy, an artist in Chicago, tells that on more than one occasion he was violently awakened from a deep sleep because his wife was ready to go. "The temperature is right and the window of opportunity is open, so wake your butt up and get to it."

Do You Do It Every Day?

You can frame that question as "Do I *get* to do it every day?" or "Do I *have* to do it every day?" In both cases, the answer is "no." Experts say that, like McDonald's, "You deserve a break today." It is recommended that you don't attempt to conceive every day. Your sperm need the rest. I'll bet you didn't even know they were tired. Seriously, though, it is thought by some to be more effective if you space your attempts every other day.

Think about it. Each time you ejaculate, you have just given the green light to 50 million sperm to begin a mad dash to reach your wife's egg. Like the Highlander says, "There can be only one." First one up the fallopian tube, to the egg, and through the membrane is the big winner. Everyone else is a loser.

Now this "don't do it every day" thing is just a theory. There is nothing stopping you from doing it once a day or several times a day. In fact, many veteran daddies believe that the amount of sex you have while trying to conceive serves to burn a vivid picture in your mind so you can remember what sex is like about ten months from now when you are as horny as a fifteen-year-old kid who just had his *National Geographic* subscription cancelled.

A side benefit to having sex every other day is that ultimately you will be able to pretty much nail down (no pun intended) the exact date of conception. This is always fun to do later when your son is sixteen and you can say "Did you know you were conceived while your mother and I were watching a variety show on the Spanish Channel at your grandma's house? Olé!" Which is sure to garner an "Ooh, yuck" from your kids … and grandma, too, should she ever discover how you defiled her couch.

The bottom line on conception, whether it happens easily or not, is to enjoy yourself. This is you and your wife expressing love for each other, and you will never have been more intimate than at this time. Enjoy it and each other, because there is a lot of work to be done over the next few months.

DADDY SMARTS TOP TIPS on CONCEPTION

- It is widely agreed that the tried and true missionary position offers the best chance for conception. Positions that are considered less effective for conception include her on top or anything involving sitting, standing, or a trapeze.
- You cannot determine the sex of your child through intercourse, diet, or other special mojo.
- If you decide to let the world know that you are trying to have a baby, people will constantly ask if you are pregnant yet, make comments, and generally poke their nose in your bedroom.
- Having constant sex in an attempt to conceive may be a lot of work, but it certainly beats the hell out of mowing the yard.
- Enjoy it—it may be a while before you have sex again.

3

We're What?

Whether it's for the first or the fifth time, learning that you are going to be a father is one of the most exciting and joyous moments in any man's life. It can also be one of the scariest. But regardless of whether you feel joy, fear, or relief, you can count on it being something you never forget.

Guys learn the big news in a variety of ways. Some are surprised (pleasantly or otherwise) by their wife or partner. Others discover it at almost the same time as their spouse. Whether you and your wife have been actively trying to conceive or it is a complete surprise, you will surely become well acquainted with a certain small, plastic device that will change your life.

Honey, Do You See a Plus Sign?

Have you ever seen the commercials for pregnancy tests? One brand shows "real" couples' reactions at the exact moment they learn they are pregnant—sort of a *Candid Camera* approach. As it turns out, they always show happy, glowing couples brought to tears of joy as the little red plus appears in the plastic square. What they neglect to show (or is probably on the editing room floor) is the couple with that "oh, shit" look of panic because they are totally unprepared for having a child.

Here is a primer for rookies being exposed to these devices for the first time. In many cases, you will be the lucky one sent to the store to retrieve one of these chemistry sets. If so, be prepared and take plenty of cash. They aren't cheap, running about ten to fifteen dollars a pop.

If you get embarrassed easily when purchasing tampons for your wife or buying condoms, then you have absolutely no business buying a pregnancy test. Jerry, a salesman in Denver, tells about buying a test for his wife. "Once when we thought we were pregnant at a very inconvenient time, I ventured off to the store to buy a test for my wife. At my local store, the pregnancy tests are in the aisle labeled Paper Towels, First Aid, and Family Planning, located right next to the condoms. I thought, 'Family Planning? What a misnomer; nothing could have been more unplanned in my life.'"

Some women are prone to going over the deep end regarding tests. They might buy several tests and keep taking them repeatedly, each time saying, "Honey, what do you see?" The test result could show the thickest, boldest, reddest negative sign you have ever seen and she will still say, "Does that look like a plus to you?" After taking several tests, she will swear that they are broken, despite the fact that the box claims 99 percent accuracy. Tests today *are* pretty accurate, but nothing is official until you get confirmation from the doctor. Then your job is to let others know.

Remember This Moment

With our first child, we had been trying to conceive for a few weeks, so when my wife was late, we had a pretty good idea that we were pregnant and decided to get a test. Little did I know that it would be up to me to purchase said test. I called my wife as I was leaving the gym after a workout and she said, "Would you mind stopping off at the drugstore and picking up a pregnancy test?"

Panic set in. This was real. In a matter of hours I was going to learn if I was going to be a father. Fifteen minutes later, I was in the drugstore wearing shorts and a bandana wrapped around my head like a pirate. At the checkout counter, the teenage clerk shot me a strange look

as he scanned my purchases: some film, a bottle of Gatorade, and, oh yeah, a pregnancy test. I went home, and I could barely get it out of the bag before Meredith had taken it from me and was headed for the bathroom, saying, "Get the camera. I'll be back in a minute."

We were rather corny about it, but you have to realize that this is one of the defining moments of your life. After you learn that you will become a father, your outlook on life will never be the same, even though the child won't be born for another nine months. This is the first of several big "wow" moments to come.

We wanted to remember the exact moment that we learned we were going to become parents. So we decided to capture it on video, just like in the stupid commercial. I set up a tripod and video camera. As Meredith brought the test out, I turned the camera on and we sat awaiting the results. When the test showed a positive result, we were able to capture our immediate reaction, joyous hysteria. In true cornball fashion, we then decided to talk into the camera and say a few words to our future baby. I realize that holding up the two-inch square of plastic and screaming, "Here you are, baby!" might have been a bit much, but I was caught up in the moment.

Whether you videotape the moment, take pictures, or write in a journal, do something to remember what you were feeling and thinking, how you and your wife reacted. Things will move pretty quickly from here on, and in five years you won't remember life without your child in the world. Refer back to these things from time to time. This was the moment it all began.

It Might Take a While to Sink In

Life is going along smoothly and regularly. You know your place in the world and then suddenly your wife says, "Honey, we're having a baby." Screeeech! Time out. Someone hit the brakes. The wheels just fell off. With one sentence your whole world just changed, and you need a moment to catch up.

Talk about big "wow" moments. This certainly qualifies as one of the biggest, and you will need a few seconds for it to sink in. It is similar to the time you asked your wife to marry you. The moment the words "Will you marry me?" came out of your mouth, your life and perspective changed forever. The difference is that when you got engaged, you were a little more in control, or at least that was what she wanted you to think.

The very first thing that some guys feel is dizziness, almost as if it isn't real. Some are overcome with emotion and start crying and laughing at the same time. Others have the stunned "deer in headlights" look and remain speechless, their mouths gaping.

On the other hand, you may actually be quite happy, but it hasn't registered yet. You know what is going on but it doesn't feel real. This is perfectly normal. After all, it is not *your* body going through changes or getting sick in the morning. You don't have a daily reminder that there is

another life coming soon. And nine months seems so far away. For many men, becoming a father doesn't fully click until four to five months into the pregnancy, when their wife becomes noticeably pregnant or when they see the ultrasound or feel the baby kick.

It can be pretty surreal. You may have just enjoyed several weeks of nonstop sex, more than you have likely had since college or your honeymoon, and the next thing you know, there is a hysterical woman crying tears of joy and holding up a plastic square with a plus sign as if it were a priceless piece of art.

Say Something

You shouldn't need any prodding or encouragement to express your unbridled joy and enthusiasm at the news, but if you are truly stunned and speechless, even from happiness, be sure to respond by saying something. Let me say this again: respond. Smile and say something—anything except, "Oh, no."

If nothing else, react for your wife's sake. It's a big moment for you, but may be even a bigger moment for your wife. This should not even be a problem, because you should be the happiest man on earth, about to jump out of your skin for joy. But remember that this moment starts the countdown to becoming a parent, and how you react right now will set the tone for the next nine months.

Telling Your Parents

Telling your parents that you are going to be a father is one of the greatest gifts a son can give his parents. Outside of telling your parents that you are getting married, this is the biggest news you will ever share with them. (Unless you count the time you told them you were dropping out of school to open a taco stand in the Virgin Islands.)

This is even bigger news than when you got married because your parents are actually participants in this. I mean, they get a whole new title. They have been your parents for twenty or thirty years or longer, and it is about time for a change in status … to grandparents. Make it a special occasion when you share the news. Even if it is on the phone, make a big deal out of it.

When we were pregnant with Samantha (our first child), we had been pressured for a good year already. "So, when are you two going to make me a grandma?" We went to Houston to visit my wife's parents. After we arrived we told her parents that we had a gift for them. My wife then handed her father a wrapped package. He removed the wrapping paper to find a package of diapers. He looked slightly confused and Meredith told him, "I think we should leave these here for the next time we visit." He clued in and became as excited as a school kid. Hugs and tears all around.

Don't Forget to Tell *Both* Sets of Parents

Generally, defer to your wife on when and how to tell the family. She may have some elaborate way that she wants to spring the news on both sets of parents. Veteran daddies agree that you and your wife should tell *both* sets of parents within the same few days if not hours. The last thing you want is for your mother-in-law with the huge mouth to become so excited at the news that she calls your mom to congratulate her, "Isn't it about time these kids had a baby?" Only to have your mom say, "What are you talking about?" Bad move, Slick. Let each set of parents hear directly from you and your wife, not from someone else. I don't care which set of parents learns first, but don't let a lot of time pass before telling both sets.

Try to tell your parents and in-laws together, as a couple. If at all possible, you and your wife should be present or at least on the phone together when telling your family. It sounds basic, but you and your wife should make the announcement together as a family.

You also want to tell your parents before you tell your friends, or at least shortly thereafter. There is cachet to being one of the first to know. Waiting until later in the pregnancy can be an insult to many parents.

What If They Don't Get Excited?

It's hard to think that your parents or your in-laws wouldn't share in your excitement, but it happens. It sucks, but it happens. Not everyone is thrilled with the idea of being a grandparent.

Just as becoming a parent confirms that you're growing up and are now a responsible adult (or at least supposed to be), becoming a grandparent can remind your parents of their own mortality. It confirms that they are growing older and that they have reached a milestone in life. Some people may think of a grandparent as someone who wears white loafers and eats dinner at 4:30 P.M. C'mon, grandparents are supposed to be old … right?

Your parents might not view themselves as old (they might not even *be* very old), so discovering that they are now in a new generational category may initially come as a shock. Eventually they will get over it, but if one or both of your parents don't jump for joy or if you hear a pregnant pause (no pun intended), don't let it throw you. Don't let their temporary selfishness spoil your joy. Focus on your wife, your child, and the type of dad you will be.

There are other reasons that a parent or in-law might not jump for joy when you spring the news that you and your wife are pregnant. If your parents don't approve of your spouse or if your in-laws hate you, they may selfishly focus their anger on you and the unborn child. Maybe they were secretly hoping that things wouldn't work out between you and your wife. Or now that there is a child on the way, your in-laws may finally realize that they aren't getting rid of you.

It's My Pity Party

If your parents live far away, their reaction may be a mix of joy and sadness. They may be happy for you, but at the same time sad or self-pitying. You may wonder, "What would Mom have to be sad about?" Well, when Mom gets that guilt engine up and running, you might hear comments like: "I won't be able to see him grow up." "We all live so far away." "I wish I could do more and be there with you." "I'll never see you all." These are all valid concerns, but don't let it bring you down. The baby is months away and you will have to deal with this issue many times during your child's life.

The things mentioned previously are real feelings that your parents might have upon learning that they will become grandparents. As frustrating as it can be, don't get mad at them. The best thing you can do is not to think about it too much or to view it as any reflection on you, your spouse, or the level of their enthusiasm or support.

Also, if your parents or an in-law says something negative to you or reacts less than enthusiastically in private, whatever you do, *don't* share this with your spouse. I'm not advocating hiding anything from her, but use your head. She is on an emotional high and thinks that everyone should be as excited as she is. A bad word or reaction from parents or in-laws at this stage can damage the relationship for the entire pregnancy. Believe me, if you think that *you* will be upset by any lack of enthusiasm on your parent's part, your spouse will be doubly upset.

Telling Siblings and Others

If there is ever an occasion that calls for a special news bulletin, this is it. This is an announcement that doesn't happen every day so you might share the news with the rest of your family in a special way like you did with your parents, assuming that you have a good relationship with them.

James in San Diego let his sister know by calling her. When she answered the phone, rather than saying "Hey, Ginni," he said, "Hey, Aunt Ginni" to see if she would pick up on it. She did. Remember, your becoming a parent affects your siblings' titles and responsibilities as well. There is great pride that comes with being an aunt or an uncle.

The moment you learn that you will be a father, you want to shout it from the rooftops, write it in the sky, and print it on billboards. It is like a great secret that you want to immediately share with everyone including friends, coworkers, and strangers. Not to put a damper on your enthusiasm, but think about holding off just a little bit before spreading the news.

Although people can announce their pregnancy at any time they choose, it is customary not to announce your pregnancy to anyone outside of family and extremely close friends until the pregnancy is at least twelve weeks along.

I've met many people who say that they are pregnant. When I ask, "How far along?" they respond, "Oh, three

weeks." You don't know squat after only three weeks. You have barely finished having sex after three weeks. There is much that can go wrong in the first trimester. The possibility of miscarriage is greatest around six to eight weeks and remains high until twelve weeks. Some faiths and cultures are even very superstitious regarding when you tell someone that you are pregnant.

Once you reach that twelve-week mark, complications can still arise throughout the pregnancy, but you have reached a milestone where it is reasonably safe to assume it is a viable pregnancy and that you can annouce it to others. Twelve weeks is the generally accepted time to wait before announcing your pregnancy to everyone.

Can We Tell Anyone Before Twelve Weeks?

It is a smart thing to tell at least your closest friend or family member before twelve weeks. Obviously, you want them to share your joy, but if something unfortunately does go wrong, such as a miscarriage, then you need a support system. A miscarriage can be devastating and highly emotional, even if the pregnancy wasn't very far along. You want to have someone to confide in who will know why you are upset. It would be unfortunate if a tragedy were to occur, and by keeping everything to yourself, you alienated your friends or family who are wondering what happened. Have a support system—but be careful about broadcasting the news on CNN just yet.

DADDY SMARTS TOP TIPS **on
DISCOVERING YOU'RE PREGNANT
AND SPREADING THE NEWS**

- Videotape the moment, take pictures, or write in a journal, but do *something* to remember what you were feeling and thinking and how you and your wife reacted.
- It might take a while to sink in. It doesn't fully click that you are to become a father until four to five months into the pregnancy, when your wife begins to be noticeably pregnant or when you see the ultrasound or feel the baby kick.
- Be sure to respond by saying something—anything except, "Oh, no." Your reaction right now will set the tone for the next nine months.
- Outside of telling your parents that you are getting married, this is the biggest news you will ever share with them. Make it a special occasion when you share the news with your parents and in-laws.
- If your parents or an in-law says something negative to you or reacts less than enthusiastically in private, whatever you do, *don't* share this with your spouse.
- The possibility for miscarriage is greatest around six to eight weeks and remains high until twelve weeks. It is customary not to announce your pregnancy to anyone outside of family and extremely close friends until the pregnancy is at least twelve weeks along.

PART 2

What Am I Going Through?

Okay, so she has to carry the baby for nine months, gain weight, and be uncomfortable, but what about me?

While everything revolves around the future mother, as it should, dads also have issues and concerns that are very real, though very different from those of moms. This section discusses things that guys are interested in during pregnancy, such as their relationships, freedom, fatherhood, money, and of course sex.

4

What Is This Going to Cost Me?

When men learn they are going to become fathers the first two thoughts they have are, "Oh my God, I'm going to be a dad," followed about five seconds later by, "Oh my God, what is this going to cost me?"

Financial concerns weigh heavily on the minds of most married men, but those concerns are magnified when you have little mouths to feed. There has likely been a financial evolution that you have seen progress as you added more responsibility to your life. When it was just you in your swinging single bachelor days, you had no one to answer to. You could work all you liked, play all you liked, and spend how you liked. Think about it—your lack of tasteful furniture and your barren fridge were evidence of this. You had no worries because no one else counted on you.

And You Thought Marriage Cost a Lot?

When you got married, things began to change. First of all, none of your furniture made the move to the new residence. I keep thinking of the movie *When Harry Met Sally,* the scene about the newlyweds arguing over the whether the wagon wheel coffee table would stay or go. As a married man, you can't spend money as indiscriminately as you once did; you need to start thinking about saving. You may begin to take your job and career much more seriously. After all, you have a wife who needs you and depends on you.

When you have a baby, it is a different story altogether. At least your wife can feed herself. On top of that, if your wife came to the marriage saddled with debt, at least she can get a job. I hate to state the obvious, but babies' earning potential is severely limited at first and their expenses make your wife's shoe fetish look paltry.

Seriously, financial concerns are another top source of anxiety for rookie dads. You may barely be making ends meet right now, and the thought of additional expenses can be frightening ... especially when you don't know what they're going to be.

When I was a rookie dad, much of the information I found was in-depth advice and analysis about investment vehicles and formulas for paying for my kid's college. It was great stuff if (a) I had a financial background and really had the time and inclination to study bonds, or (b) I had enough money to worry about buying bonds.

The fact is that not every rookie dad has a stash to invest. If you do, then I recommend talking with your broker, financial planner, accountant, or adviser to prepare for your child's birth, education, and financial future. Because money matters are so personal and every family's goals are so different, you need the advice of a professional planner.

Regardless of your financial situation, every rookie needs to know what costs he can expect and a few tips that can make his life easier once the baby arrives.

Get Your Financial House in Order

One of the first things you should do is to get your financial life in order. I know it can take time, but fortunately, you have several months to prepare.

Try to pay off any credit card debt you may have. At the very least, try to obtain a cheaper rate or transfer the balances to a card with a better interest rate. You might start by getting rid of store cards and specialty cards, which carry the highest interest rates.

When you sit down to pay bills each month, do you write so many checks that you clear a forest with the paper used? Chances are, you could save time and money by consolidating many of your bills. Talk to your bank about a consolidation loan to pay off credit cards with one check and get a better interest rate.

Look at what bills could be paid with automatic debits and what companies offer multiple services so you can double up and don't have to write multiple checks. Writing checks every month may not seem like a hassle right now, but believe me, when your baby comes you will need every spare minute. Things will be hectic and you don't want to risk letting a bill slip through the cracks.

You might be surprised at how much money you waste. Even if you're loaded, you can't afford to burn money now. You've got a child to think about. Look for places to cut expenses. I'm not talking about living on an austerity budget or saving money by cutting your hair with a vacuum cleaner—simply identify areas and services that you pay for but aren't getting full value from.

Your television cable and satellite services are a great place to identify waste. We did this and saved a good amount of money. I looked at the additional sports and movie channels we subscribed to. We had the ultimate couch-potato package that cost a small fortune every month. But did we really watch Billy Bob's Fishing Channel, the Monster Truck Network, and Canadian sports that even ESPN2 won't cover? No, so I cut 'em. Result: about $20 saved per month. Certainly not a fortune, but $240 a year buys a month and a half of baby formula or two months of diapers or can pay for twelve nights of babysitting, which you and your wife might really appreciate.

Plan a Budget Without Your Wife's Salary

If your spouse works, at some point you need to discuss your child care options and your wife's career plans. If she chooses not to return to work, you need to calculate a family budget that does not include her salary. You may be relying upon that extra income, so this may not even be feasible. However, you have to realize that even if your wife chooses not to work, this isn't necessarily a negative thing. Forget for a moment the benefits of having a stay-at-home parent; let's look at this from a strictly financial perspective.

Say that your wife's monthly net salary (after taxes, retirement, insurance, etc.) is $2,000. Once the baby arrives, there will be additional expenses. You will have to pay for day care if your wife is to work full time, which can cost anywhere from $600 on up a month. If she commutes, assume $100 a month for gas or transportation, which is on top of her commuting time. Unless she is in a casual work environment, she could have dry cleaning and clothing expenses of $100 a month. If she eats lunch out regularly, she is spending $100 a month, calculated at $5 a day. These

are just a few of the actual monthly costs associated with going to work.

Of course, corners can be cut—rides shared and brown-bag lunches taken. But considering expenses, your wife's take-home salary is $1,100 a month, not the $2,000 you had expected. The net effect may be that your wife's income isn't significant enough to warrant her working full time or sending your child to day care. I'm not advocating one way or another. Each family and each woman is different. However, if this is something you are considering, you should perform this financial exercise.

I have said that you should calculate a budget without your wife's salary, but there is a growing trend for men to forego their careers and become stay-at-home dads. However, it is still more common for women to make the choice to stay at home after the birth of a child. If your wife is the lead careerist and breadwinner and you wish to be a stay-at-home parent, then by all means calculate the budget by eliminating your own salary.

So, What's It Going to Cost Me?

You are looking at three kinds of costs: (a) preparing for baby; (b) hospital and birth; (c) after baby.

Preparing for Baby Before the baby arrives, your main costs will be preparing a nursery and purchasing all the baby's equipment, such as cradle, changing table, rocker and other furniture, car seat, and stroller. Fortunately, you will receive much of this equipment, with the exception of furniture, from your wife's baby shower. However, don't count on getting it all. Your wife may not have a baby shower, in which case you will have to pick up all the expenses. You can spend an unlimited amount on decorating a nursery, and equipment comes in all levels and prices, but you can expect to spend a minimum of $500 to $1,000. Car seats alone cost close to $100.

If you are on a budget, one way you can defray some of these costs is to borrow certain items from friends and family. Your wife has probably beaten you to the punch here, but if your sister has already had her two kids and her strollers are sitting in the garage, then ask if you can borrow them. It is a shame that baby stuff is so expensive, because you use it for such a short amount of time. Look to your friends whose kids are about three or four years old and who aren't planning on having any more children. Chances are their stuff is in the attic, and they would be happy to let you borrow it.

Hospital and Birth What does it really cost to have a baby? It depends on the type of birth you have.

It isn't like you get much of an option on which type of birth you want. The more common, preferred, and cheaper method of birth is vaginal, but complications or health reasons may necessitate a Cesarean, or C-section.

Childbirth is not like ordering from an a la carte menu, so it is tough to say exactly what the costs will be.

They can vary from hospital to hospital and state to state, and depend upon the circumstances of the actual birth. Costs can also vary according to the health of your wife and child.

You can expect an uncomplicated vaginal birth and hospital stay to cost between $2,000 and $5,000. If a C-section is required, the costs can go up considerably. The cost of a Cesarean birth can range from $5,000 to $10,000. If there are complications or problems with the child that require admission to the intensive care unit, the cost will far exceed that figure. Costs can also skyrocket if the baby needs to remain in the hospital for an extended period of time after birth, as is common with extremely premature babies.

Now that you've caught your breath and come to terms with the idea that Junior is already putting you several grand in the hole and he isn't even home yet, relax, take a deep breath, and thank God (and your employer or your wife's employer) for insurance.

If you and your wife both work and have insurance plans, then you should take a hard look at both packages to determine which one you want to use. Don't take for granted that your plan is the best or that it even covers childbirth. Some employers exclude that option from their health plans or make it an add-on expense. Check it out beforehand.

Regardless of whose insurance plan you choose, if it covers childbirth you can expect it to handle anywhere from 50 to 100 percent of the total costs. When our children were born, our plan covered 90 percent of the costs of the birth, hospital stay, and care for my wife and babies. My responsibility was 10 percent of the bill, so I owed approximately $600 when we left the hospital. That I could handle, and to put icing on top, the hospital took American Express, so I got frequent flyer miles. Thanks, kids.

Birth is certainly expensive and insurance helps defray much of the cost, but if you aren't insured, and even if you are, most hospitals will work out a payment plan. So you don't have to write a big check or sell the furniture to bring your baby home.

After Baby Don't put that wallet up yet, Dad. You aren't through. Here are a few costs to consider once you get baby home.

Car

One of the great scenes from the movie *Nine Months* with Hugh Grant is when he has to give up his beautiful Porsche for a (gasp) family car.

Research shows that the safest place in a car for children under twelve, especially infants, is in the back seat. Unless your work requires it, you may want to think about giving up that truck or two seater.

You need to take stock of your current automobile and determine whether it is reliable and safe. If not, you should consider trading it in. I'm not saying to buy a new car—like you need another expense—but to look at a newer, larger model that you, your wife, and baby (and all of baby's gear) can travel in safely and comfortably.

A family car doesn't have to be a giant land yacht or a minivan, although I hear minivans drive quite nicely. (I wouldn't be caught dead in one, but you may choose to.) It may be time for your taste in automobiles to grow up. You can still have a cool ride with four doors.

■

Allen, an engineer in Kansas City, had driven Mustangs since he was in high school. When his wife became pregnant, he was reluctant to give up the car. "It has a back seat," he argued. When he finally tried to put a car seat in the cramped back compartment, he knew that his two-door sports car days were numbered. He eventually joined the four-door club. (For the record, I'm a Ford SUV guy.)

Babysitters

Unless you have a family member or friend who will watch your kids for free, you can count on adding another $20–$40 on top of the dinner and movie. Babysitter rates vary widely depending on what part of the country you live in, but you can figure on $5 to $10 an hour.

Food

If your wife chooses to breast-feed, food is free for about a year. If she chooses not to or cannot breast-feed, you will begin to look upon formula as liquid gold. Simply put, the stuff ain't cheap. And depending on your child's appetite, you can go through a ton of it.

Formula comes in premixed liquid or powdered form. While brands and sizes vary, formula costs $60 to $90 a case. A case can consist of two large cans, each weighing two pounds. This will last you anywhere from two to three weeks, depending upon your child. With my son Skylar, who is a future offensive lineman, we went through two cases a month at $87 each. This will continue until your child starts eating cereal (mushy cereal, not Wheaties) in two to six months, or soft table food or baby food from a jar in six to nine months.

Diapers and Accessories

This is another area where we can just hook up a direct link from your wallet to the store. Disposable diaper prices vary according to brand and the package size you choose. Packages come with as few as eighteen diapers and as many as seventy-two. The cost ranges from $9 to $25. Children go through anywhere from six to twelve diapers a day for the first few months.

You also have to figure on spending money for bottles, wipes, pacifiers, and baby shampoo, although these are minor in comparison.

Clothes

For the first few months, all babies wear little gowns, which you've hopefully received plenty of at the baby shower. You can spend as much as you like on baby clothes. You will find that an outfit the size of one of your socks can cost more than one of your nicest shirts. Just remember that a baby is just as likely to spit up on a fifty-dollar outfit from Neiman Marcus as she is on a five-dollar outfit from Target.

You can find cute clothing at plenty of places without spending a fortune. The Gap, Old Navy, and Gymboree have great baby items at reasonable prices, in the $10 to $30 range. But you can also find many everyday outfits and great baby bargains under $10 at Target, Babies R Us, Wal Mart, and other discounters such as Mervyn's California, Ross, and TJ Maxx.

The clothing expenses you need to think about are your own. Your own dry cleaning will dramatically increase. I'm serious. You will find more stains, spills, and spots that you can't identify than you ever have in your life. And usually you will find them just before you go into a meeting or out for the night.

Day Care

There are many options for day care, and costs vary upon the type of care and what part of the country you live in. Birmingham is cheaper than Dallas and Dallas is cheaper than New York. Regardless of the type of care you choose, you can expect to pay between $400 to $1,200 per month per child. If you have an in-house nanny, it can be even more.

DADDY SMARTS TOP TIPS on
WHAT THIS IS GOING TO COST YOU

- Get your financial house in order.
- Try to consolidate and pay bills in advance so you don't have to worry about writing checks when the baby comes.
- If your wife chooses not to return to work, you will need to calculate a family budget that does not include her salary.
- You can expect an uncomplicated vaginal birth and hospital stay to cost from $2,000 to $5,000. If a C-section is required, the costs can go up considerably. The cost of a Cesarean birth can range from $5,000 to $10,000.
- If you and your wife are covered, determine whose insurance you want to use. Don't take for granted that your plan is the best or that it even covers childbirth. Some employers exclude birth from their health plans or make it an add-on expense.
- Most hospitals will work out a payment plan, so you don't have to write a big check or sell the furniture to bring your baby home.

5

Doctor's Visits

Up to this point in your adult life, you have probably never gone to the doctor *with* anyone other than your parents. But now is different. You are part of a team. You are like a coach who has a vested interest in his player's health and is constantly quizzing the trainer or doctor.

Generally, your wife will visit her obstetrician/gynecologist (OB/GYN) every month until about the thirty-second week. From thirty-two weeks until the final month, she will go to the doctor every other week. During the last month before the birth of your child, she will see her doctor every week. These appointments are mandatory.

Do I Have to Go to Every Appointment?

If you can make time *and* your wife wants you there, the *Daddy Smart* thing to do would be to attend every appointment. You will certainly score points showing your wife that you are supportive. It is also a great way to get involved and feel like a participant in the pregnancy. In addition, you will learn firsthand what is going on with Mom and baby. If this is your first child, then I suggest going to as many of the appointments as she is comfortable having you at.

Not every appointment is a "gee, wow" experience. Toward the end of the pregnancy, when your wife is going to the doctor every other week (and then every week), not much changes from one visit to the next. If you can only go to a few doctor's visits with your wife, there are three that you absolutely shouldn't miss.

Discovering You're Pregnant

With the widespread availability of home pregnancy tests, many women have a pretty good idea before they go to the doctor whether or not they are expecting. But the "official" visit is still a huge event. This can happen any time within the first trimester but generally happens within the first eight weeks.

Hearing the Baby's Heart Beat

Usually around ten to fourteen weeks, you will be able to hear the baby's heart beat for the first time. This is one of the first "big wow" moments after learning that you will become parents. It is really the first contact you will have with your child. It can be very moving to men, but this visit really seems to impact Mom. It is confirmation that something is really living inside of her. Guys tend be more visual and are moved by the sonogram or ultrasound.

Sonogram/Ultrasound

Somewhere between the sixteenth and twentieth weeks, you will have the opportunity to see your baby for the first time. Through an ultrasound or sonogram, a noninvasive procedure performed in the doctor's office, you will be able to see your baby's features and organs. This is the visit where most people learn whether or not they are having a boy or a girl, if they choose to find out.

Of all of the trips to the doctor, this is a "don't miss" visit. In the movie *Nine Months*, (a *Daddy Smart* must-see), Hugh Grant misses the sonogram appointment because he is playing tennis and thus spends the rest of the movie getting out of the doghouse. You *do not* want to miss this one for the obvious reason that it will upset your wife. But more important, this is the first time you will see your baby.

This is something you definitely want to experience in person and be able to share with your wife. Video-tape is not a good substitute here. You want to be there. For most guys this is the moment when everything becomes real; it suddenly dawns on them that they will become a father.

Important Additional Visits

Occasionally, certain problems and concerns can occur that require additional doctor's appointments, sometimes with a specialist. The most common reasons for these additional non-emergency visits are so that amniocentesis and level 2 ultrasound may be performed.

Amniocentesis (or "amnio," as it is often called) is a test that is generally performed between the sixteenth and eighteenth weeks of pregnancy. It is a highly accurate test of a woman's amniotic fluid that can diagnose or rule out certain birth defects. It is used most commonly to identify genetic and chromosomal disorders such as Down's syndrome and neural tube defects like spina bifida. The test also accurately identifies the sex of your child.

It is considered an invasive procedure with a risk of miscarriage. The fact that a long needle is inserted into your wife's stomach to collect the amniotic fluid and can come in contact with the baby, along with the possible ramifications of the test's results, can be overwhelming. You should try to attend to reassure and help your wife. She will require bed rest for a day or two afterward to minimize the risk of infection or miscarriage. (Read more in Part 3, "What She Is Going Through.")

Other than regularly scheduled

appointments, any time your wife experiences a complication or problem such as extreme pain, bleeding, or spotting, or if she has not felt the baby move in a while—which can occur late in the pregnancy—then a special trip to the doctor or even the emergency room may be required. You should drop everything and go with her when this happens. It may turn out to be nothing at all, but she will likely be scared and will need you for support.

After the birth of your child, unless your wife is having difficulty such as bleeding, she will return to her OB/GYN after six weeks for a routine maintenance visit. There is no strong need for you to go on this visit or any others after the baby is born.

There is a good chance that your wife's doctor is male. If so, you can always hope that he is some old grandfatherly figure and not someone who looks like George Clooney, Noah Wyle, or some other TV stud doctor. But as luck would have it, he may end up being a regular guy, which can be disconcerting to many men.

One of the main reasons guys don't want to attend appointments with their wives is because they have a problem with being in the room when their wife is examined. Much of the exam is routine such as checking weight, blood pressure, and measurements. But later in the pregnancy comes the internal exam. This is when many guys lose it.

Not the Three-Way You Had in Mind

C'mon, you have to admit that it is a little strange to be three feet away from where a doctor has his hands several inches inside your wife and the three of you are having a conversation like nothing's going on. The only person for whom this might not appear so odd is the doctor, but only because he has done it a few thousand times and nothing shocks him.

It can be a very strange scenario, but compared to the actual labor and delivery, this is only one of the preliminaries. You can stay for the entire exam, but if you are uncomfortable during the actual pelvic examination, then by all means leave the room, stand behind a curtain or just look away. Your wife will pick up on your nervousness.

While we are on this subject, it should be mentioned that if your wife's doctor is a man, you should quickly get over any jealous or delusional thoughts about an examination being sexual in nature. I'm sure that every twelve-year-old boy in the world fantasizes about becoming a gynecologist once he learns what the word means. However, as the gynecologist father of one of my childhood friends once said, "They all pretty much look the same."

Forget for a moment what is being examined. It is about as glamorous and sexy as going to the dentist. If you were to turn the tables, I seriously doubt that your wife harbors any jealous or sexual thoughts when you are being checked for a hernia or go for your annual prostate exam. These men and women are professionals, and regardless of how hot or special your wife is, don't you think the doctor is a bit jaded? Bottom line: get over it.

Of course, all of this is really up to your wife. If she isn't comfortable with you in the room, then all bets are off. Before you invite yourself to anything, ask your wife if she would like you to go with her and how much of your participation she is comfortable with.

Shana, a mommy in Dallas, talked about her anxiety when her husband came to one of her early doctor's visits. "It wasn't the exam itself that bothered me, but the last thing I wanted was to step on the scale and have my husband looking over my shoulder. I said, 'Get the hell away from here.'"

You Are Along for the Ride

Realize that regardless of whether your wife's doctor is a man or a woman, you will not exist. Smart doctors will get to know you, be pleasant and answer any questions you may have. At the very minimum, the doctor will at least acknowledge your presence. But remember that he or she is there for your wife, not for you. You are merely an accessory. Although the doctor may explain things to you both, the doctor's primary relationship is with your wife.

Smart Stuff for Getting Along with Your Doctor

Other than you, her doctor will be the most important person in your wife's life for the next nine months, not to mention the person who will likely be bringing your child into the world. Therefore, it is important for you to feel comfortable around them.

Make it a point to get to know your wife's OB/GYN. Knowing a little bit about the person who will be taking care of your wife and bringing your child into the world will set you at ease. You obviously want someone who is a skilled doctor, but it sure helps if he or she is personable, makes an effort to know you, and cares about your wife's emotional as well as physical well-being. This is critical on Labor Day since you may have to make sure that your wife's wishes are respected and she doesn't get bullied or run over by a doctor.

While most doctors are sensitive and caring, not every one has a wonderful bedside manner. Veteran daddies agree that if there is a problem on Labor Day, it is much easier to communicate with your wife's doctor if you have at least met him, rather than venting on a stranger in an already emotionally charged situation.

He's Your Wife's Doctor, Not Yours

There is a rapport between your wife and her doctor. Don't be surprised if your wife even has an admiration or mildly flirty relationship with her doctor. I'm convinced that guys are in awe of OB/GYNs because we feel that they know some special way to turn any woman into jelly, and they probably do, but the point is that these people are professionals.

You want your wife to have a great deal of faith and trust in this person and to feel completely comfortable with her doctor's technical abilities and capacity to care.

All guys are different. You may be right there, driving your wife to her doctor's appointments and offering to help the doctor, or you may feel like scheduling an out-of-town trip when they occur. The point is that you support your wife. You don't have to attend every appointment, but go to the milestone appointments. You will regret it if you don't. You may be uncomfortable with doctor's offices, hospitals, and what is being discussed, but it is all in preparation for the big day.

DADDY SMARTS TOP TIPS on DOCTOR'S VISITS

- Go to as many appointments as your wife is comfortable having you at.
- If you can only go to a few doctor's visits with your wife, there are three that you absolutely shouldn't miss: when you learn that you are pregnant; hearing the baby's heartbeat for the first time; the sonogram.
- Get to know your wife's doctor.
- Remember that the doctor is there for your wife, not for you.

6

Who Are You and What Have You Done with My Wife?

When people think of the stereotypical pregnant woman, often what comes to mind is either someone who is weepy, emotional, and irrational or someone who is highly irritable, emotional, and irrational. (And how is this behavior different from every other day, you might ask?)

If they haven't already, these phrases will soon become part of your lexicon: "Why don't you get back on your broom and fly away?"; "I don't know who you are anymore"; "Why are you crying?"; "What is wrong?"; "I'm sorry"; and of course, "What did I do now?"

J.A.D.A.—Just Another Dumbass

I don't care if you are a success in business, managing millions of dollars and thousands of employees by day. You can save lives or pilot a multimillion-dollar aircraft from one end of the globe to the other. When your wife is pregnant, you are just another dumbass who can't do anything right.

C'mon, it's easy to make light of the mood swings of a pregnant woman. Moodiness during pregnancy is as inevitable as death and taxes. It is going to happen, no matter how much of a princess your wife is. We joke about women's emotions, temper, and moods during pregnancy much as we do about PMS. It is funny to everyone … except her—and the husband who has to live with her for nine months.

I've read all the books for men on pregnancy and heard tips from the experts, both men and women, on how to deal with your wife's tender emotions. Every book or article gently jokes about the stress that pregnancy puts on a relationship and consistently advises men to simply "agree with everything your wife says." One book, by a guy whose fathering experience I suspect was limited to a test tube, seriously offered this groundbreaking relationship advice: "Stay away from commenting on her weight or the size of her butt."

World's Greatest Understatement: "Pregnancy Will Test Your Relationship"

Most "experts" also downplay the severity and frequency of mood swings. Kind of like when the dentist says, "You will experience some discomfort," just as he is about to grind the drill into your molars. The experts said it would be tough, but they never said that it would be so inconsistent and volatile. They also didn't tell me that it would last for as long as it did. I was under the impression that only the first trimester was tough on the relationship. By the eighth month, I was starting to think something was wrong.

Even the most stable men have a hard time dealing with the Jekyll-and-Hyde tendencies their wives display. Sadness, joy, fear, or anger; it is a coin flip to determine which you will encounter from day to day and week to week. The truth is that regardless of how strong your marriage is and how much you love your wife, there will be times when you will wonder if you really know this person or if it will last. All joking aside, it is a serious concern for most men and can cause conflict, confusion, and in extreme cases depression and a visible strain on your marriage.

It is important to note that every woman reacts to pregnancy differently. I sincerely hope that your wife is happy, glowing and on an even keel for nine months straight. The mood swings and emotions described here don't apply to every woman, but based on experience and conversations with veteran daddies in researching this book, they apply to most.

Just Agree with Everything Your Wife Says—Yeah, Right

As I said, the most common advice for getting along with your wife during pregnancy is to simply agree with everything she says. It is good advice in principle; it just isn't realistic. I would like to meet the man who can genuinely agree with his wife on everything for nine months and still pee standing up. Not to say that constantly agreeing with your wife means you are a wuss. I agree quite frequently. Hey, I'm no dummy. I like where I sleep. But we are men, and traditionally think that we have a pretty good handle on how things should or shouldn't be done.

This is certainly not meant to condone a Cro-Magnon, sexist mentality. It is just realistic and natural that there will be some conflict. There is not a man in America able to keep his mouth shut and agree with everything his wife says for nine months. It just isn't happening, especially given some of the irrational arguments and hormonal tantrums he will encounter.

I know this may not be pleasant to hear, but I'm telling it like it is, brother. I don't want to sugar coat it for you. Your relationship *will* change during this period. You *will* fight and you *will* be wrong regardless of how salient your points are or how much the facts are in your favor.

But I'm *Right*

No, you're not. Get this through

your head. *You will not be right for quite some time.* But the point isn't to be right. You do not get a prize for winning an argument with a pregnant woman. You get pain, tears, heartache, and the couch.

When both of you are on an even playing ground, meaning that she is not pregnant and isn't supercharged on hormones, you can defend a point and use logic to try to win the argument. However, the rules have now changed. In this situation, your goal is not be right or win the argument. *It is to avoid a major blow-up.* Being right or fighting to the death on principle is fruitless, futile, and stupid.

Every woman is different, but here are several possible causes behind her behavior, along with some things she may ask you to get for her.

Get Me Some Painkillers

Her body is changing. She is not just uncomfortable but in some cases is in serious pain. Her body is going through rapid changes that we as guys have never even considered.

I remember my wife telling me how her hips and joints were in excruciating pain and she could feel them moving and separating. We joke around about "breeder hips," but women's bones (including their hips) actually get wider and spread apart in preparation for delivering the child.

Get Me a New Body, an Air Conditioner, and a Nap

Think about where her organs have to go. Everything is shoved up into her rib cage because the baby is now where her stomach used to be.

She is constantly tired not only from carrying around the extra weight of baby, blood, fluids, and fat, but from the drain of the baby literally feeding off of her and taking nutrients. She is also hot, and I don't mean as in looking. She will feel physically hot and sweaty, requiring your home to stay as cold as a meat locker. Consider that she is constantly on the verge of peeing in her pants because "your child" is dancing on top of her bladder; you might be a little bitchy, too.

Get Me a Harpoon

At times during her pregnancy you could fit your wife's self-esteem into a thimble. She is forgetful, which pisses her off no end because she feels stupid. She may feel badly about how she looks and what this is doing to her body. While we may think that she is glowing, beautiful, and sexier than ever, your wife feels like she is wearing a tent and could perform the ten o'clock whale show at Sea World.

Get Me a Gold Medal ... or At Least Some Gold Jewelry

I asked my wife and other veteran moms what advice they have for future fathers on how to deal with a pregnant woman. The answers were clear, consistent, and decisive: "Stay out of my way and be prepared for me to blame you for anything and everything including *my having to carry your child.*" Okay, guys. Are we all clear on that?

As far as women are concerned, they are doing us a huge favor by carrying our seed, and they will go to great lengths to remind us of that fact

… for the rest of our lives. Forget that in some cases they were the ones begging to become pregnant. That doesn't matter because it was you and your errant penis that inflicted her with this condition. You jerk.

It's a Competition

In addition, women compete in ways that guys aren't aware of. They ask seemingly innocent questions of each other and drop small comparisons in an effort to see who is the superior mother. "How much have you gained? Really? Oh, when I was pregnant, I gained only twenty pounds and I lost my weight in three weeks. I also ran a marathon a month after I gave birth. Did I mention my labor was only three hours and I only had to push once? Is your husband involved with the pregnancy? Oh. My husband was in the delivery room. In fact he cut the cord … with his teeth."

You don't understand how much pressure this puts on your wife. She feels that she must be this super-woman who does it all, who has an easy birth, an involved husband, a beautiful baby, and looks great immediately after a twenty-two-hour labor without drugs. This competition continues after the baby is born. (More on this in Part Six: "Labor Day."

Get Me a Divorce Attorney

There are times when her thought process will be in an irrational downward spiral to disaster. You are at the filling station putting gas in your wife's car when she looks over and sees a young woman at the next pump. Suddenly she thinks that you are going to leave her for the surgically enhanced PYT (Pretty Young Thing) in the Daisy Duke cutoffs pumping gas next to you. Your wife pictures herself in five years, left alone with a child, a fat single mother who has to eat cat food and live under the freeway. And here you are in Aruba with a Dallas Cowboys cheerleader. You bastard—how could you do that to her? Meanwhile, you put the gas cap back on, get in the car to find your wife sobbing, and wonder what you could have possibly done.

Get Away from Me

People are constantly pawing her. Once she starts to show, her tummy becomes public property and everyone will want to pat her stomach like checking to see if a watermelon is ripe. She will be so sick of being touched that if you want to keep that hand, you had better remove it from her ASAP.

Get Me a Trash Can

She is constantly nauseated. Familiar smells and foods that she has always loved now make her hurl like a frat boy at a keg party. One daddy I spoke with, Glenn, said his wife would become so violently ill whenever she smelled common bath soap that she couldn't be around him after he showered.

Get Me a Tissue

Your wife could be as tough as nails but will now inexplicably erupt into sobs at the sight of a Michelin commercial, a Kodak moment, or a Discovery Channel documentary. My wife never really cries, but once during her second pregnancy, I walked in while she was watching *Beverly Hills 90210* and she was crying as if she had lost a loved one. When I asked why she was crying, she laughed and said, "I have no idea."

I'll Have a Double Hormone Martini

There are many reasons for this behavior, but at the root is the incredible hormonal cocktail that is coursing through her system. This is not meant to open up a wave of stereotypical PMS jokes, but the mood swings and temperament of pregnancy are not that different than those of PMS … except that it lasts for almost a year. That's right, buddy. You thought just nine months? Sorry. You can expect your wife to be affected like this in varying degrees throughout the entire pregnancy, and possibly about six weeks to three months after birth, until her hormones and body get back to normal.

Is This Going to Change Our Relationship?

Some guys are scared of becoming a father not because they fear caring for a child, but because they fear their relationship with their wife will always be this rocky. This is one reason that men are reluctant to get involved in the pregnancy. It is tough to get excited and geared up about sharing this experience when the person you're closest to is acting like public enemy number one.

One reason that a partner's emotions and mood swings can be so upsetting is that you are already wondering if having a child will change your relationship for the worse. Here the baby hasn't even arrived yet and your marriage has taken on a completely different dynamic.

Sadly, the term of pregnancy isn't necessarily a change for the better. You don't even recognize or in some cases even like your wife. Pregnancy does change your relationship. This is tough to handle for even the most confident and loving husband. You're thinking, "If this is how she is going to be for the rest of our lives, I want no part of this."

Now don't get me wrong. This has absolutely nothing to do with love and commitment. The love, commitment, and stability are always there, or at least should be. As you may have already discovered, good marriages take hard work and aren't always about candlelit dinners and romantic walks on the beach. What you will encounter during pregnancy will test your patience and communication skills. But it is during this time that you will be forged into a family.

How to Have Peace, Love, and Harmony … and Still Feel Like a Man

As you have figured out, I am a pragmatist. I'm not going to naively tell you that simply putting on a smile and agreeing with everything your wife says or does for nine months will spare you from getting yelled at or being confused.

There will be times when it doesn't matter what you say or do. Your wife will be sad, mad, or scared, and there is nothing you can do to make it better. Pregnant women get and deserve a great deal of latitude, but a handful of women view pregnancy as a license to say and do anything, and anyone in their path be damned. "Oh, give me a break. I'm pregnant." As if they were suddenly unable to control the venom spewing from their mouths. The people who often bear the brunt of this verbal lashing are their husbands. This is the dark part of pregnancy for men that no one really discusses because we want to focus on the happy parts or joke around about moodiness.

I spoke with veteran daddies who bit their tongues throughout the entire pregnancy, never voicing any of their thoughts or concerns about the family, being a father, or their relationship. Thinking they were doing the right thing by remaining silent, their frustration ultimately turned into resentment, which they carried inside throughout the pregnancy. Ultimately, it spoiled their experience.

The keys to getting along during pregnancy are communication and picking your battles. The "experts" are right in principle: you *should* agree with your wife and go out of your way to make her happy. That means you don't have to make a federal case of everything or fight to the death on every little detail. The goal is to take care of your wife, protect her, and avoid blowups and any unnecessary stress. There are times when you are just going to have bite the bullet and

say, "Okay. You're right." Would you rather be happy or right?

When Enough Is Enough

However, despite what your wife is going through, there is a limit. Having a baby is not a license to disrespect or walk on you. She is doing 99.5 percent of the work right now, but you are a family and this is your pregnancy too. After all, you are still going to have to live with this woman afterward.

When she seems to be out of control or says something that sends you into orbit, try to step back and determine if there is some other reason she is acting this way. Is it genuinely the hormones talking? Is she sad or scared? Or has she just crossed the line? Knowing the reason can help you determine how (and whether) to react. If you choose to respond, wait until you have both cooled down and then calmly tell her what you were thinking or feeling.

Whatever you do in the heat of battle, do not walk out without saying anything. ("Up yours" doesn't count.) As I've pointed out, she may already have irrational fears that you are going to leave her with this baby, and your storming out the door does not help.

When you are at the end of your rope it is okay to blow off steam. Recognizing that you need some time to cool off and decompress is just as important as actually doing so. Go to the gym, go for a run, shoot baskets, hit golf balls, anything that will get you out of the house and let you think about something other than pregnancy, fatherhood, and work.

Talk to Guys Who Can Identify with What You're Going Through

Sometimes it is also good for you to have other guys you can talk to about this. Actually, my wife and her best friend *were pregnant at the same time.* Her husband Steve and I would get together regularly to vent about what was going on in "hormone land," compare notes, or just talk about anything unrelated to wives, work, or kids. If this is your first child, don't expect your single buddies to really understand. It is probably best to vent to a veteran dad with a little experience and mileage.

If you are now so scared that you have booked the ticket to Aruba and are looking for a Dallas Cowboys cheerleader to accompany you, don't pack the bags just yet. It gets better. I promise. You just have to be patient.

Guys are often scared to talk much about their relationship at home during pregnancy. We may gripe and bitch to our closest buddies, but guys really don't share a lot of these problems or concerns. We tend to think something is wrong with us or even our marriage.

Despite What You Think, She Is Not Satan

Hear this. There is nothing wrong with your marriage. It is normal. Every guy experiences this. You did not marry Satan and you did not make a bad choice. The only bad choice will be if you do something

rash or stupid during pregnancy, like stray or be mean to or alienate your wife and unborn child. Lastly, it will not always be like this. This too shall pass, and in time you might even choose to go through it again.

DADDY SMARTS TOP TIPS **on WHY YOUR WIFE IS ACTING THIS WAY**

- **Every woman reacts to pregnancy differently.**
- **Your relationship *will* change during this period. You *will* fight and you *will* be wrong regardless of how salient your points are or how the facts favor you.**
- **Your wife may be in a foul mood because of hormones or because she is uncomfortable, scared, nauseated, hot, feeling unattractive, and concerned for her own health and that of the baby.**
- **It does get better. There is nothing wrong with your marriage. This too shall pass.**
- **Pick your battles. Being right or fighting to the death on principle with a pregnant woman is fruitless and stupid. Your goal is not be right or win the argument. *It is to avoid a major blowup.***
- **Talk to veteran dads and guys who can identify with what you're going through.**
- **Despite what you think, your wife is not Satan.**

7

Thanks for the Advice ... Now Shut Up

People have had children for thousands of years. As a rookie, you will find out that there are plenty of people with much more experience and knowledge than you. Unfortunately, many of these people feel it is their duty, if not God-given right, to tell you and your wife exactly what you should be doing—and that what you *are* doing is certainly wrong.

It is not just in-laws, friends, and family members who offer unsolicited advice. Everyone has to put up with a certain amount of unsolicited family grief. It's the price you pay. What you are probably not used to is the amount of nagging, nudging, and nosiness that goes on from total strangers. You will have complete strangers offering dos and don'ts and asking for intimate details you aren't comfortable discussing with your physician or clergy, let alone with someone you've met in line at the movies.

And You Thought You Had It Bad

Fortunately, guys don't have to deal with nearly as much grief as women do. You will be simply amazed at what people will say to you and your wife, but it is your wife who bears the brunt of these verbal onslaughts. It doesn't matter whether it is a relative or a stranger, the comments can be brutal. Frankly, men could never be pregnant because they would resort to fisticuffs if someone were to talk to them the way pregnant women are spoken to.

Many comments are delivered under the guise of "helpful advice," and some are genuinely helpful and well-meaning. However, some are just stupid, thoughtless, or mean.

People will comment to your wife about her weight, her health, her stomach, her choice of names, and her choice of doctors, hospitals, and nursery designs. She will be criticized for gaining too much weight or not enough. She will be openly reprimanded by total strangers for ordering certain foods in a restaurant, or yelled at for doing something usually perceived as healthy, such as working out. She will be ostracized in public for attempting to pick up anything over five pounds.

People will question her judgment on child care options as well as her choice to stay home or return to work. She will be critiqued and offered advice on her choice to breast-feed and whether or not to breast-feed in public. If she chooses to use formula instead of breast-feeding, she will receive a brow beating from breast-feeding supporters whose kids are still on the teat at age six. (I think that when your kids can ask for it, they might be too old to breast-feed).

Without thinking, people will upset your wife by talking about pregnancy horror stories or what can go wrong during labor. She will even be criticized about you: you travel too much, you should be doing more to help, you should be making more money so she doesn't have to work. My point is that there is a lot of advice out there, and like it or not, you will get a big dose of it.

Excuse Me—Can I See Some ID?

Your primary job is to protect your wife. Think of yourself as a bouncer at a club, making sure no one gets out of hand. People will be insensitive and say stupid things without thinking. You need to make sure that no one treads on her or you and be a supporter when everyone is telling her what she is doing is wrong or is second-guessing her decisions.

Take advice only from people you respect. When strangers offer opinions or advice, simply take what makes sense and forget the rest. Everyone has different lifestyles, circumstances, beliefs, and preferences. If you two have made decisions about your family, the child, and how you will raise it, then don't let others sway you or doubt yourself. Stick to your guns and do what is right for you and your family.

It's hard to believe that with so many people forcing advice upon you, there will still be times when you need someone to turn to for information, answers, or simply to vent. Since you won't know half of the people offering their sage advice and might not trust the other half, it is important that you find someone whom you consider to be a mentor or role model. This can be your own dad, your father-in-law, a brother, or a close buddy or coworker who is a veteran daddy. It can even be the husband of one of your wife's friends, assuming they have kids who aren't mutants. Having this person act as your parenting Yoda will give you a release and a source of information you can trust.

You Have the Right to Remain Silent

You aren't compelled to tell every stranger (or every family member, for that matter) what your choices are, or every detail of your pregnancy. Simply stating "We don't know," "We haven't decided yet," "It is a surprise," or "We've decided not to tell anyone" is a great way to get someone off of your back and deflect intrusive questions.

If a stranger goes over the line, politely change the subject or turn away. If he or she persists, then lead your wife away from them and when she is out of earshot, *then* lay into the person. Don't make a huge scene in front of your wife or draw attention to her.

In-Laws—"Have You Seen *Throw Momma from the Train*?"

As I said, much of the advice and comments are directed at your wife, but believe me, you won't get off easy. Frankly, there isn't that much a stranger can say that will upset you, and the only comments your buddies might make are cracks about how you aren't seeing much action at home. Even siblings and fathers-in-law don't really interfere. Nope, your ears will receive a beating from your mother-in-law and other female relatives.

Let me go on record by saying that I have a wonderful mother-in-law. She was an invaluable help throughout both pregnancies and remains a loving help to this day. We are lucky to have her. She knows her limits, and understands that there can be such a thing as too much family time.

Seriously, the only challenge is that she sometimes thinks that I'm wearing a big T-shirt that says, "Ask Me, I'm the Shell Answer Man," because she will ask me questions about my wife that I couldn't possibly know the answer to. "Bradley, where did Meredith get this blouse and how much did she pay? Was it on sale? Do

you know if they have it in red?" But otherwise my mother-in-law experience has been great, and she loves me a lot. Other daddies, however, warn that you and your wife will need to set some ground rules early when it comes to family advice.

For many mothers in-law, and even for your own mother, your wife's pregnancy is viewed as a great opportunity to relive their own and to allow them to feel truly useful and needed. And part of what they need is to tell you what to do. Your mother-in-law is concerned about her baby (your wife), and wants to know that she is being taken care of, especially if she can't be there or lives in another part of the country. We tend to forget about our own moms, but they may be as involved if not more so than a mother-in-law, especially if she did not have a daughter or if there is no other family nearby.

What Are You Doing to Help My Little Girl, You Slacker?

Mama bear is going to expect you to take care of her little girl. You will be quizzed: Is she eating? Why isn't she gaining weight? Why is she lifting that? Why are you letting her work so much? Why isn't she drinking her orange juice? Is she taking her vitamins? And if she isn't taking them, you can count on it that mother-in-law has an idea about how you should get your wife to take them.

Part of this just comes with the territory and should be taken with a grain of salt, a nod, and a "sure, whatever you say." There is no reason that you should become a punching bag for things that are totally beyond your control.

Set, Communicate, and Enforce the Ground Rules

You and your wife need to establish boundaries for your mother-in-law, or for any relative for that matter. If someone like your mother-in-law has stepped over the line or is disrespectful to you, keep your cool and take her aside, away from your wife.

Tell her that you appreciate her help and advice and that both of you have your wife's best interest in mind and only want her to be happy, healthy, and stress-free. If she has a question about your wife's behavior, then she should ask your wife directly. You are trying as best you know how, and if there is a problem, then you're sure that your wife will tell you.

You have to be careful here because you don't want to alienate your mother-in-law or any other family member. You also don't want this to happen in front of your wife, which would upset her. If it persists or gets out of control to the point where the family member is abusive to you or overly demanding in front of your wife, then it is okay to mention this.

Beware of "Super Dad"

While the type of advice that dads tend to give one another has to do with pretty generic and superficial stuff such as "get some sleep, you'll need it," there is a rare breed of "Super Dad." These men are usually very touchy-feely types who likely beat drums, read *Iron John,* and hug trees. They are the type who, when they learn you are a dad or are going to become a father, feel they need to give you a profile of their kids, complete with a play-by-play description of each child's birth, worthy of an ESPN *SportsCenter* highlight reel.

I encountered a Super Dad on a flight back from California. If you are like me, you cherish your airplane time. No phone calls or meetings mean that I'm able to get a great deal of work done, so I'm not big on socializing in flight.

My seatmate was craning his neck to look at my laptop computer screen. "Hey, are you doing some work?"

"Yes," I answered.

"What are you working on?" I knew then that he was a talker, and much as I wanted to tell him I was working on a terrorist plot, I politely answered his question. He then asked me if I had any children. I warmed up a little and discovered that he too had kids. Their ages were thirteen years, ten years, and two months. I said, "Wow. That's a big difference in ages. What was it like having them that far apart?"

He was in his early forties, the type of earthy guy who wears Birkenstocks with socks and listens to a lot of Grateful Dead. "It's beautiful, man. We had the baby at home and got the kids involved." I thought, okay, home births are not that common, but it isn't like giving birth in a barn or anything. It is simply a matter of preference.

I asked, "A home birth? How was that?" Wrong question.

He responded with, "Oh man, it was great. We did an *underwater* home birth." Now underwater births *are* a little out there. It is supposed to be easier on Mom. The water supports her weight and the baby is introduced into a warm environment similar to the womb.

I thought, I'll bite. "So where did you have it?" He said they had it in the hot tub. "You mean the hot tub in your backyard or your bathroom?"

"No, man, we moved the hot tub into our living room with everyone there. Our kids were there and they watched."

"You mean they saw from a distance?"

"No, man, they were right there and saw the baby come out and everything. Beautiful experience."

As I smiled and turned my head toward my computer, I thought, "Yuck!" I don't know which grossed me out more: the thought of this guy's hot tub being turned into after-birth soup or the thought of his thirteen-year-old witnessing every graphic detail of his mother giving birth. TMI: Too much information.

DADDY SMARTS TOP TIPS **on UNSOLICITED ADVICE**

- Everyone has opinions and advice on how you and your wife should go through pregnancy and raise your kids. Take what makes sense and don't worry about the rest.
- You aren't compelled to tell every stranger, or every family member, for that matter, what your choices are or every detail of your pregnancy.

8

Sex—Oh Yeah, I Remember That

You and your spouse have likely mated like wild rabbits in order to become pregnant. You have had more sex than you can ever remember. Sexually speaking, you have been going ninety miles an hour with your hair on fire, the scenery screaming by, and then suddenly … screech! Someone throws the emergency brake and everything comes to a sudden stop.

Depending on whom you talk to, sexual experiences during pregnancy can vary widely. However, they can generally be characterized as feast or famine. Most veteran daddies agree that there is little that is regular about pregnant sex, either in frequency or style. In fact, you can generally count on it taking a good nine to eighteen months for your sex life to get back to normal.

Just as every woman responds to pregnancy differently, every woman views sex during pregnancy differently. Here are some guidelines regarding pregnant sex that every guy needs to know.

She's Gotta Have It

Some guys talk about how their wives simply cannot get enough sex during pregnancy. I don't know any of these guys, but I hear they exist. This generally happens in the second trimester, after she is over morning sickness and is starting to feel a little more like herself. The changing chemistry and hormones that occur in women during pregnancy make each one respond differently. In some women, it means that they have an increased sex drive.

If you are lucky enough to have your wife feel good physically, good about the way she looks, and sexy, then congratulations—enjoy it. As is to be expected, there is an incredible emotional bond that is intensified during pregnancy and that is only heightened as you and your wife make love during this time. When you do get together, it will be something very special.

The Drought

While some women just gotta have it, the opposite is much more common. Many veteran daddies say the reason you get so much sex while trying to conceive is so you can remember what it is like for the next nine months.

Don't be surprised if your wife's sex drive is diminished, if not non-existent. In the beginning, or first trimester, she is likely to be continually nauseated. Later in the pregnancy, she will be physically uncomfortable or unhappy with her looks. If this is the case, the last thing on her mind will be sex.

This can wreak havoc on guys who find their wives have never looked sexier and more beautiful than when pregnant. If you talk to most guys they will tell you that there is something incredibly appealing and sexy about their wives when they are pregnant. Some men find their wives' new, larger, more curvaceous bodies incredibly sexy.

People commonly refer to a pregnant woman as "glowing," and it's true. Part of it has to do with her excitement about being pregnant, her increased bloodflow, and overall healthy, alive look, but it is also likely due to the fact that pregnancy has given her more shapely curves. Your wife may have gained some weight, but that weight gain has likely made her breasts fuller and her figure more curvaceous. It's a matter of preference; some guys find this fuller feminine look very attractive, while others are turned off.

If the latter is the case, then lack of sex might not be a crushing blow for you. But daddies agree that if you like where you sleep, keep your mouth shut. She will lose the weight once the baby is born. Some women lose it faster than others, but she will have her own motivation for getting it off and your reminding her will only make her feel worse and put unnecessary strain on your relationship.

Whether you and your wife are as busy as rabbits or your sex life is in hibernation, you may have many concerns about sex during and after pregnancy. We guys think we finally have a handle on married sex, have gotten into a great routine, know what goes where and what the other likes, and suddenly the rules change. Here are a few of the common concerns that guys have about pregnant sex and their wives' changing bodies.

How Frequently Can We Have Sex?

As much or little as she wants to. It really is up to her. As long as she feels like having sex, it is physically possible to have sex right up until the due date. It will not do your wife or the baby any harm. In fact, around the due date, having sex is recommended as one way to induce labor.

A chemical found in semen helps thin the cervix and speed up labor, so doctors recommend having sex if you are past your due date. Experts also recommend walking and eating Mexican food, but I like this better. The challenge here is actually having sex. After forty weeks, you might be safer approaching a rabid dog than attempting to have sex with a pregnant woman who is tired, has a sore back, aching nipples, and hemorrhoids, and is lugging around at least an extra thirty pounds.

Why Are You So Cranky?

Your wife, friends, or coworkers may ask you this at some point during the pregnancy. I realize that *she* is the one who is supposed to be cranky and irritable, but after a lengthy dry spell without sex, sometimes lasting months, it is common for guys to become as sexually frustrated as a pimply-faced teenager. It's not only sex; she may not want you to touch her in *any* way, shape, or form. If you are affectionate or used to a lot of contact, this may be difficult for you.

Don't worry, guys, her lack of interest in sex, affection, or contact has nothing to do with you and is not a statement on your marriage. This is important to remember because many guys take it personally. As a result, they unintentionally heap guilt on their wife about the lack of action in the bedroom. Remember that she probably feels bad enough and is very aware of the fact that you two haven't been together in a while, but the last thing she needs is to feel guilty because you are being deprived. Believe me, this will not help your situation.

Veteran daddies say the best thing to do when you are frustrated is to work out, lift weights, shoot hoops, hit golf balls, or go for a run. Replace one physical activity for another. Jerrod, a veteran daddy in New York, says, "During both of my wife's pregnancies, I went for so many walks and runs I felt like Kane from *Kung Fu* wandering the earth."

Will I Hurt the Baby?

No. Don't worry, you aren't alone. Every guy has thought this or had creepy visions of poking his child in the head, hurting the child, piercing the amniotic sac, or having the baby grab him from the inside. Creepy, but that's what some guys think.

First of all, it physically can't happen. The baby is too far up the birth canal to be in contact with your penis … no matter how gifted you are. So, unless you are Dirk Diggler or Secretariat, check your ego at the door.

Common sense says that you shouldn't do any deep thrusting, anything overly physical or that involves a running start. Otherwise, go for it and enjoy it while you can. The only way you can hurt your baby is by lying on top of your wife's big belly with your own big belly. Which leads me to my next topic …

The Geometry of Pregnant Sex

For at least the first four or maybe five months, if you're lucky enough to have sex when she isn't sick or tired, or the two of you aren't fighting, it's really not that different than normal. Your bodies fit together as they always have. Your usual and favorite positions will work, barring any unusual gymnastics. It is at about month five and beyond, when your wife is really beginning to show, that sex requires a great deal of thought and strategy.

I will tell you that pregnant sex

may not be the best, wildest, most passionate, or hottest experience you have ever had, but it sure is one of the most fun and entertaining. It is a lot like sexual Twister. You will end up laughing uncontrollably as you try to be romantic or intimate and realize that there is this huge basketball that keeps getting in the way.

About the eighth month, if you and your spouse are trying to have sex, you will need a team of NASA engineers to help calculate your point of entry. All kidding aside, if you are going to make it work, you can just forget the missionary position. It is not only difficult unless you are standing and she is lying down, but it can seriously harm your wife and the child if you put your whole weight on your wife. Don't risk it. As far as from behind, some people claim that the angle and position of her uterus can make this uncomfortable for a pregnant woman. The veteran daddies' position of choice is to have your wife on top. It is not only easier on her, but it's great fun and you do less of the work.

Will Sex Be the Same After the Baby?

This is a common concern. While we like to think we know how the female equipment works, we are hardly gynecologists. A lot of guys think that sex won't feel the same after a woman gives birth, especially given the fact that an object roughly the size of a large football has just passed through her vagina. Since chances are pretty good that you are

not gifted enough to be equipped with a football-sized penis or even a pool-cue-sized penis, in some cases you might wonder how you will ever again measure up (no pun intended).

The fact is that the vagina is remarkably elastic. It is meant to go back to its original size and shape after delivering a baby, and yes, that means accommodating you. After a few weeks, everything is back to normal. However, her soreness may persist for a while, especially if she had an episiotomy (a surgical cut enlarging the vagina so the baby may pass more easily) or experienced vaginal tearing during birth, both of which require stitches. The bottom line is not to worry; you won't be rendered inadequate, useless, or less than able in the bedroom.

Pulling Back the Wizard's Curtain

In the movie *The Wizard of Oz*, everyone is in awe of the great and powerful Oz. But when Toto pulls back the wizard's curtain to reveal a small man and machinery instead of a powerful wizard, the illusion is shattered. For a handful of guys, witnessing the actual birthing event is similar to watching the wizard's curtain pulled back. Seeing the blood, the fluids, and the baby, while amazing, is one of the least sexual experiences you can go through, despite the fact that you and everyone else in the room are staring squarely between your wife's legs. Chances are that you will not even recognize what you are looking at.

For some guys this can remain a major hang-up long after the baby is born and your wife's body has returned to normal. They have a difficult time getting over the "functionality" of the female body. If this is the case, first of all, try to get over the fact that you think of your wife's body as something belonging to you. Your wife is beautiful and is the same person you fell in love with and found incredibly sexy before having children. However, right now her body is functioning exactly as intended to produce and protect your child. Things will return to normal. If you think that this may become a problem and worry that watching the birth will change your view of sex in any way, then do yourself and your wife a favor, and don't watch.

I Can't Sleep with Her ... She's Someone's Mom

Before pregnancy, your sex life may have been as wild, hot, and tawdry as a B movie on Cinemax. But now that your wife is pregnant, you see her in a different light. You can't possibly do *those* things with her now. After all, she's someone's mother.

Some guys actually get hung up on the idea that now that she is a mother, she is no longer a sexual being. In fact, she is still the same woman you found attractive. However, she obviously isn't the Virgin Mary either. The fact that you and your wife are now responsible parents doesn't mean that your sex life has to be beige and boring. Having sex does not make you bad parents. You might

have to stop hanging from the trapeze in your bedroom, but otherwise, don't let the fact that your wife is a mother change how you respond to each other.

Since it may have been a while since you and your wife have actually had sex, it may be a little tense when you finally get back in the swing of things. Part of that tension may come from uneasiness on her part because of her new body. She may be very self-conscious and nervous about being naked in front of you, especially since her body may look dramatically different.

Part of the uneasiness may also come from your not knowing how to react to your wife's new body, the fact that you haven't been together in a while, or that you both may have been under a lot of emotional pressure. Just relax. She isn't expecting fireworks, and neither should you.

Water, Water Everywhere but Not a Drop to Drink

Yes, your wife's body looks dramatically different, and part of that transformation is her breasts. One of the great side benefits of pregnancy is that your wife's breasts will increase in size. Increased breast size and sensitivity is often one of the first signs of pregnancy.

Your wife's new surgery-free breasts may be delightful to look at and you may have your own plans about how much fun that they will be to play with. However, in what seems to be one of the great ironies of pregnancy, these giant breasts that are so appealing are going to be completely off limits. Let me repeat this so it sinks in for you, guys. You can look … but don't touch.

Sad but true. Many women's breasts will be sore. Your wife's nipples will be extrasensitive to the slightest touch, let alone any rigorous sexual activity. To make matters even more confusing: late in the pregnancy, as her breasts prepare to produce milk, they will begin to ooze a clear milky substance called colostrum, a nutrient-rich form of early breast milk. This can be a bit unsettling for guys who aren't expecting it and have viewed breasts as recreational rather than functional items up to this point.

The bottom line is that during pregnancy your love for your wife will grow and develop in ways you've never imagined. Whether sexual or emotional, communication and understanding are the keys to strengthening your relationship and reaching that next stage in your evolution as a couple: parenthood.

DADDY SMARTS TOP TIPS **on SEX DURING PREGNANCY**

- Sexual experience during pregnancy can generally be characterized as feast or famine.
- You can generally count on it taking a good nine to eighteen months for your sex life to get back to normal.
- As long as she feels like having sex, it is physically possible to have sex right up until the due date. It will not do your wife or the baby any harm.
- Don't worry, guys, her lack of interest in sex, affection, or contact has nothing to do with you and is not a statement on your marriage.
- If you are frustrated, go work out, lift weights, shoot hoops, hit golf balls, or go for a run. Replace one physical activity with another.
- About the eighth month, if you and your spouse are trying to have sex you will need a team of NASA engineers to help calculate your point of entry.
- Women's bodies are remarkably elastic, and a few weeks after giving birth, your wife's body will return to normal. After your wife gives birth to a child, you won't be rendered inadequate, useless, or inept in the bedroom.
- A handful of guys have a difficult time getting over the "functionality" of the female body. Your wife is beautiful and is the same person you fell in love with and found incredibly sexy before having children. However, right now her body is functioning exactly as intended to produce and protect your child.

Hey, What About Me?

feel like I'm pregnant, too" is a comment future daddies frequently make. (Hopefully, not because their stomachs are expanding like their wife's.) But despite the fact that it is also your life, relationship, and home that are going to change due to the new baby, everyone caters to pregnant women.

Think about it. They get all the perks. They get their own special maternity clothes, they get special parking spots at the grocery store, they don't have to do any heavy lifting, and they get to gain weight and not care. Sure, they have to do some heavy pushing after nine months, but in the meantime, people throw parties in their honor and give them lots of free stuff, and they get doted on and pampered for nine months. What a deal.

All kidding aside, pregnancy and childbirth is an ongoing celebration of women, children, and life itself … as it should be. But with all of the attention heaped on Mom and baby-to-be, not to mention mom's moodiness and temperament, old Dad can begin to feel a bit alienated, left out in the cold, and pretty much like a mere sperm donor.

Your wife will and should be the focal point of the pregnancy. That is the way the system is set up. She doesn't have to do anything except sit there glowing and quietly expanding while she is lavished with attention.

Parenting is considered a partnership, a joint activity to include the participation of both mother and father. Pregnancy, on the other hand, is a different matter. Men are certainly participants in the beginning, or at least for a solid fifteen minutes, as we pass on our genetic code. After that and the announcement that you are becoming a father, the focus is firmly on your wife and child until you are asked to pay the bill nine months later.

I'm not saying that guys aren't involved. Each man is different in the amount he wants to participate. You may be the type of guy that doesn't want to draw any attention to yourself and are content to let your wife take care of everything related to baby. Much like many married guys' social life, pregnancy can quickly become "Just tell me where I have to be and when" if you aren't careful.

Many guys view fatherhood as something that starts once the baby is born; everything else is *her* experience. In this veteran dad's opinion, that is an outdated way of thinking. I don't say this to come across as "Mr. Modern Sensitive Family Man." I'm saying that fatherhood and the fathering experience start long before the baby is born, and not becoming fully involved in the pregnancy not only cheats your wife, but cheats *you* out of an incredible experience that you will be lucky enough to have only a few times in your life, maybe only once.

To the Outside World, You Don't Exist

At first people will heap congratulations on you, but shortly after the words leave their mouths, they are talking to Mom, which is where the focus will be throughout pregnancy and for a while after the baby arrives. You are not going to be the center of attention during pregnancy, so get used to people asking your wife anything baby-related. People will stop asking about *you*. All questions will be about your wife, the baby, and the nursery. This is preparation for when your parents and in-laws come to see the baby and immediately pass by you and your wife, screaming, "Hi. Now, where's that cute little baby?"

It is easy to feel left out and a little like a spectator when it is your wife who has this life growing inside of her and is experiencing all the changes internally and externally. Women naturally have a stronger bond to the child in the beginning. This is one of the great things that women have on us guys. It isn't even like this is a competition and it bothers us that they do something better than we can; they do something that we just *can't*. We can't even fathom what it is like. We can make a cabinet or a free throw, but we can't make a baby.

The fact is, some guys have rough time with this. They become detached or even jealous of their wife's relationship with the unborn baby. They see their wife as giving their child life. They see themselves as observers. If there is little communication between husband and wife, the situation is aggravated. And I'm here to tell you if you are having trouble dealing with this now, then just wait until breastfeeding. More stuff that men can't do … although I don't know why you would want to.

Don't think that pregnancy is only your wife's experience. You can be as involved with the child and pregnancy as you want to be. Do not shut yourself out or allow anyone else to prevent you from being as much a part of this experience as you would like. This is the first step in making the transition from couple to family.

How to Get Involved

One of the most common complaints from pregnant women, outside of discomfort, is that they wish their husbands were more involved and excited about the pregnancy. Too many guys display indifference simply because they don't know how to get involved. As any veteran daddy can tell you, if you show the slightest interest or excitement in the baby and the pregnancy, not only will your stock with your wife go through the roof and your status be elevated as the best husband among all her friends, but she will be happy to let you into the game.

By taking a few of the following hints, you will not only become involved and bond with your baby but you will score major points with your wife and feel that you are in the game rather than on the bench.

Don't guess or wonder about your wife is going through or why something is happening with her body—ask her. Ask what she is going through, how she feels, and what she is thinking. If you miss a doctor's appointment or choose not to go, ask her what happened. Ask questions about the baby and its development. Ask her what things feel like.

You will be surprised and amazed at her description of what the baby's kicks feel like, what it is like to have the baby roll inside of her stomach, or what the pressure on her lower back and organs is like because the baby has moved into a new position. Ask her what it feels like when the baby responds to certain things she eats. Every aspect is fascinating, especially if you are a science buff. This will become your entertainment. I'm

telling you, it's better than the Nature Channel.

Once the baby begins to kick and move around, there really is nothing more fascinating than watching the pokes, prods, and waves coming from inside your wife's stomach. Late in the pregnancy, it looks like something from *Alien*.

As it turns out, many babies sleep during the day because Mom's walking rocks them to sleep. When Mom finally lies down, the baby wakes up; thinking that it is time to play, the baby will start to move around. After a while you will be able to guess what body part is sticking out and determine if it is an elbow, a foot, a head, or a little bony bottom that is trying to poke through.

Craig, a real estate developer in Denver, says: "My wife and I made a game of it. Every night before we went to bed, we would just watch her stomach and try to guess what part was moving. Watching my baby move inside of my wife's stomach made it all seem even more real to me, even more so than the ultrasound. The baby would move at certain times and roll a certain way, which helped us start to learn our baby's habits and personality."

In addition to watching your baby move around, you can actually have conversations with your child. Surprisingly, babies can respond to voices, music, and other noises while still inside the womb.

It may feel strange to talk to your

wife's stomach, and believe me, talking to a navel that is sticking out like a meat thermometer is recommended for only the most confident man. But bear in mind this is something I suggest you do only in the privacy of your own home. Tell your baby about your day. Try reading stories to your baby. My wife and I read books and talked to all our babies every night before going to bed. Play your favorite music for your child.

It doesn't matter what you say or do, just talk to your baby regularly. You will feel like a dork at first, but I guarantee that the first time you can feel or see the baby move or respond to your voice, you will be hooked. I spoke a lot to Samantha while she was in the womb, and I swear she knew my voice as soon as she was born. Whether it had to do with my talking to her in the womb, I don't know. But I do know that by speaking to her for months, I felt a special bond with her before she was born. When we finally met and she responded to my voice, I fell in love instantly.

If you know the sex and have selected a name, then call the baby by name. When my first child was born, we knew it was a girl and we had already selected a name, so for the last trimester, I spoke directly to Samantha. With our second child, we chose not to learn the sex, so I just referred to the child as "Little Bean." Feel free to choose your own dorky name.

At first your wife may ask if you would like to talk to the baby. Do it. It will show her that you want to get to know your child and will put her at ease. After you get used to it, don't wait for your wife to ask you to speak to the baby. If you feel like speaking to your baby, then do it—after receiving permission.

Permission to Approach the Tummy, Your Honor

Yes, it is your child, but we have already discussed your wife's tummy being treated like public property. Sometimes she won't want you or anyone else near her. If you want to talk to the baby, don't just walk up to your wife and place your face on her stomach. Ask her if you can talk to the baby right then. If she seems cranky or tired, recognize that she may need some space. Cut her some slack and ask again later.

Brush Up on the Subject

You are off to a great start by reading this book. But if you really want in-depth or technical information about what is going on with your wife and baby, then try reading some of her books. Two of the best are *What to Expect When You're Expecting* and *The Girlfriend's Guide to Pregnancy.*

Write down everything that happens, from the time you learn that you're going to be a father to the moment you hear your baby's first cry. There are plenty of formal journals and diaries for women, but you don't need anything fancy or structured. Just buy a notebook or keep your journal on your computer. This is something you and your wife can look back on and even show your kids later. But most of all it is for you to work through much of what you are experiencing.

At the beginning of each month, write a letter to your baby. I know that your child may be brilliant, but I doubt she will pop out of the womb reading. These letters are more for you. However, you can keep this tradition up as your child grows older and present the collected letters as a gift on a significant birthday like her sixteenth or twenty-first, or even way down the road when your child becomes a father or mother.

Keeping House

You might not care whether or not your child's room has a Winnie the Pooh motif or a stars and moon theme, and you might not have much choice if you do care, but you can be involved by helping to prepare the house for baby's arrival. Simple ways include putting furniture together, helping to make the house baby-proof, or cleaning out the spare room. Plant flowers. Make a sunny reading nook or clear out an area in the garden or back yard where your wife can sit and confortably feed the child. (See "Getting the House Ready for Baby."

■

David, a reporter in Tampa, says: "We had a spare room that held all of our junk and boxes that we didn't have room for. My wife and I had talked about cleaning it out someday, but the baby's arrival was a good motivator. As I cleaned out the room to make way for a nursery, I felt like I was actually doing something for my child."

Work up your postbaby budget. Calculate your finances without your wife's salary (or yours). Start to research investments, mutual funds, trusts, or savings options once your child is born. Beef up your life insurance.

Make Something for Your Child

You don't have to be Bob Vila or some super handyman, but you can get involved in the pregnancy and preparations for your baby by simply putting up shelves or painting a room, or more complex, by building a toy-chest. Another idea is to create or refurbish something that can be passed down to your child as an heirloom to start a tradition.

■

Bill, a consultant in New Jersey, says: "My mother had a miniature wooden rocking chair that her father had made for her when she was a small child. I found it in my grandmother's house after she passed away, only three months before my daughter was born. The paint was chipped and faded. I was saddened that my daughter would never get to know my grandparents, but I saw the chair as a way to share that legacy. I took it home and spent time preparing the chair and repainting it for my daughter."

Go to Doctor's Appointments

Get involved by getting informed. Go to your wife's doctor's visits or at least to the important ones that she wants you there for. You will not only support your wife but you will learn everything that is going on with your child, and you can ask the doctor if you have any questions. Read "Doctor's Visits," to get the full scoop.

Be Around Kids and Practice on Friends' Children

Try to spend time with friends or relatives who have children. If they have an infant, volunteer to baby-sit. Your wife will be on board with this because she gets to be around a cute baby, and your friends will appreciate having a free baby-sitter. Practice changing a diaper and holding and feeding a child before your big day comes. The good part is that you can give *this* child back at the end of the night or when you are tired of the crying.

Keep a Picture of the Sonogram

Show people a picture of your baby. Ask the technician if you can have a copy of the sonogram. All he or she has to do is hit a button to print a picture that you can take with you. This is your first baby picture. You will find yourself proudly showing people this black-and-white picture of a blob like it is a studio portrait. The paper is similar to old rolled-type fax paper, so be sure to preserve it in a frame or scrapbook.

I'm a big fan of framing the picture and displaying it. I still keep framed

sonogram pictures of my kids in my office today. I have my daughter's framed sonogram on a shelf next to pictures of her at various ages. These are the ultimate before-and-after photos.

Who Is Fred and What Is He Doing in Our Bed?

If you haven't started to feel a little neglected in other areas of your life, there is one area where I can guarantee you will be squeezed out ... your bed. I'm not talking about sex here, although that is certainly a possibility. I'm talking about the fact that there will be less room in your bed, and not just because your wife is bigger.

Basically, her sleep habits will change throughout pregnancy. Obviously, she is larger, and she may feel hotter at times. She may shove all the covers onto your side or simply take the covers off the bed. Most guys can deal with that.

However, because of her added girth she will find it difficult to sleep in positions she found comfortable before. After a certain point, there simply won't be any way for her to sleep on her stomach. Because she needs to find some way to support her stomach while sleeping, she may surround herself with pillows while sleeping. These pillows may be beneath her back or stomach or they may be shoved between her legs, anything she needs to do for support.

What this means is that if you and your wife had been "spooners," that is, if you liked to sleep next to one another cuddled like spoons in a drawer, you can forget about it. There will be a barrier between you and your wife, and frankly, she needs those pillows more than she needs you.

While some women opt for many pillows, others choose what is called a body pillow. Body pillows look like regular bed pillows except they are about four feet long. Most women end up hugging the pillow or wrapping it around their bodies or under their stomachs for support. If you are looking for a great cheap gift for your wife, go to a department store, Bed Bath & Beyond, or any bedding store to buy her a body pillow. You will be a king.

The downside is that you will kick yourself a few weeks afterward when you realize you have replaced yourself with a four-foot pillow that now rests where you used to sleep ... next

to your wife. Between the five full-sized pillows and the four-foot body pillow my wife slept with, there was little room for me. I pretended to grow resentful of the body pillow and named him Fred, because I told my wife it was like having a four-foot man in our bed. Occasionally, we would have pillow fights and I would pretend to beat up Fred for moving in on my wife.

There Is Just More of Me to Love

A lot of men try to identify with their wife during pregnancy. One negative way of doing this is by gaining weight with them. Of course this is not done intentionally, but if your wife is eating anything and everything, then it is a little harder for you to stick to a diet or regimen. My wife

TOP TV FATHERS

Most TV fathers are perfect, loving, and always make the right decision, but they never show Ward giving the Beaver a time-out, do they? Which top TV dad are you most like?

Bill Cosby	Cosby Show (Mmm, Jell-O pudding, anyone?)
Ward Cleaver	Leave It to Beaver
Ozzie Nelson	Ozzie and Harriet
Philip Drummond	Different Strokes
Fred Sanford	Sanford & Son
Andy Griffith	The Andy Griffith Show (Aunt Bea frightens me.)
Robert Young	Father Knows Best
Homer Simpson	The Simpsons
Al Bundy	Married with Children
Brian Keith	Family Affair (Technically not a dad, a very cool uncle)
Bob Saget	Full House
Bill Bixby	The Courtship of Eddie's Father (Piss off dad, and he turns into the Incredible Hulk)
Dick Van Patten	Eight Is Enough (Hey, Dick. Two words: birth control.)
Mike Brady	Brady Bunch (He's an architect and their house has one bathroom for eight people. Think about it.)

would send me out to the ice cream store, and there was just no way I could come back with one cone. C'mon, I couldn't let her eat alone.

The only problem here is that while she gains weight, at the end of the nine months she automatically loses much of it in the form of a baby. At the end of your nine-month growth period, I doubt you are going to give birth to a nine-pound burrito grande.

This weight gain is but one symptom of couvade, that is, sympathetic pregnancy. Others include moodiness and nausea. While these may be very real, they are often a subconscious way for men to shift the focus of the pregnancy onto themselves. It doesn't happen to all guys and it can last just a few weeks to several months, any time during the pregnancy.

Baby Showers

While you've likely never attended one, most guys are familiar with the concept of a baby shower. A baby shower is simply a party held in honor of your wife and baby. The mother-to-be receives gifts in preparation for the baby's arrival. These showers may be large or small affairs and your wife may even have several showers given by different people. Her coworkers may have a shower one week, followed by another hosted by her close friends, sister, or other family members.

Why is this important to you? It's pretty unlikely that you will even attend and you could care less about a cute little ruffled onesie that a room-

ful of women are cooing and oohing over. Well, it's important for one very important reason, brother: it's *free stuff.*

Let me put this another way. Baby gear is expensive. Small clothes come with a big price. Little butts require many diapers. Babies require special car seats, strollers, and multiple beds—cradles, bassinets, cribs—and other furniture items you can't identity and never thought you would buy.

The bottom line is that all of these things cost money ... a lot of money. If your friends, family, acquaintances, and perfect strangers give you things that you don't have to spend money on, then it is like Christmas in July.

Besides getting free gear, another reason you should care is because baby showers are a big deal to your wife. So you should be aware of when they are, who is hosting them for her, and what she receives. A smart thing would be to send flowers to your wife at her shower or send a gift she can open in front of her friends.

In some places, especially the South, there is a growing trend to have a "couple's baby shower." It is essentially the same thing as a regular baby shower except the men are forced to endure an evening of "oh, it's so cute" and pressure from their wives about having children.

Actually, couple's showers can be pretty fun if they are done creatively. Some people play baby-oriented games such as "Pregnant Pictionary." One interesting game often played at couple's showers involves giving a diaper pin to everyone when they arrive. You are to place the pin on your shirt or lapel. Throughout the evening whenever anyone mentions the word "baby," they must surrender their pin to the person who heard them say it. The person who collects the most diaper pins at the end of the evening wins.

DADDY SMARTS TOP TIPS **on GETTING INVOLVED IN THE PREGNANCY**

- It is perfectly normal for you to feel a bit alienated, left out in the cold, and pretty much like a mere sperm donor.
- Don't think that pregnancy is just your wife's experience. You can be as involved with the child and pregnancy, as you want to be. Don't shut yourself out or allow anyone else to prevent you from being as much a part of this experience as you would like.
- If you show the slightest interest or excitement in the baby and the pregnancy, your stock with your wife will go through the roof and your status will be elevated as the best husband among all of her friends.
- Don't guess or wonder what your wife is going through or why something is happening with her body, ask her.
- Ask to watch the baby kick and move in your wife's stomach. Talk to your unborn baby. Babies can respond to voices, music, and other noises while still inside the womb.
- Read everything you can about pregnancy and babies.
- Keep a journal.
- Write a letter to your child.
- Take care of the house.
- Make something for your child.
- Go to your wife's doctor's appointments.
- Baby-sit for friends' kids to get used to being around children.
- Keep a picture of the sonogram in your office or wallet.

10

What Kind of Dad Will I Be?

At some point during the pregnancy, you will begin to ponder what type of father you will be. You may take a look at other dads when you are at the mall or a restaurant and picture yourself with your own child. You may even catch yourself daydreaming about playing catch with your son or swinging your little girl at the park.

If this is your first child, you are venturing into uncharted territory. But even if this is your second or third child, both you and your wife will find yourselves wondering what type of parents you will be and how this child will affect you.

While you and your wife will share some of the common issues and thoughts, such as wondering what your baby will look like, wondering what type of father you will be is one of the greatest sources of anxiety for men.

This Isn't Your Father's Fatherhood

What it means to be a father has changed significantly since the time when most of us were children. There really isn't a standard stereotype for what a father should be today. In over 60 percent of American households, both parents work full time, which means that dads play a much more active role around the house and with the kids than our fathers ever did.

In fact, demographers, sociologists, and generational experts anticipate that today's generation of young men will be excellent fathers. Men in their twenties and thirties today were often raised by "Baby Boomer" fathers who were workaholics. Sacrifices had to be made for the Boomers' careers, and it was often the family that paid the price.

Over half of twenty- and thirty-somethings today are also the products of divorce. On top of that, this group was the first generation of latchkey kids, unsupervised children whose mothers worked full time outside of the house. This lack of attention to children and instability in the home has had a significant impact on those young adults who are now becoming parents. Many have sworn they will do things differently, take a greater role in their children's lives, and be the fathers they wish their dads had been.

Until this point in your life, you most likely haven't thought much about becoming a father. Actually, you have probably tried to avoid thinking about it. But now that fatherhood is imminent, you will start to think about the changes going on in your life and how your every action will affect another human being. For many guys, this is an opportunity to reflect on their own childhood and to think about their own fathers.

Most of what we know about fatherhood we've learned from our own fathers. In and of itself, this can be a great source of either strength or fear for most guys—your own frame of reference and upbringing will have a lot to do with which. Actually, this can be a difficult struggle for many guys. Will I be like my father, and more important, is that a good or a bad thing?

Whether your father was a positive or negative role model, use him as a road map to determine what type of father you do or don't want to become. Look no further than your own childhood to determine what strengths you want to adopt from your father and which characteristics you wish to avoid.

For men who are close to their fathers and admire them, their dads serve as role models, someone to emulate and pattern themselves after. But this can also be a burden for men who put undue pressure on themselves to live up to their fathers.

What If My Dad Wasn't a Good Role Model?

Growing up, if a man didn't have a close relationship with his father, or his father was either abusive or simply not around, deciding what type of father to become can be even more confusing. This situation is more common than you might expect, since over half of the men in their twenties and thirties today are products of divorce; their exposure to their fathers was often limited to summers and every other weekend. Their fathers were the last of the "organization men" who put company ahead of family. This has had an impact on many men who are becoming first-time fathers today. Fear of being like their father is often one of the reasons for men to postpone having children. Other men who did not have good relationships with their dads can't wait to have kids so they can "do things right."

Many veteran daddies say they coped with the fear of becoming like their fathers by overcompensating. They thought, "If my dad was a workaholic who was always on the road, I'm going to find a less demanding job and be there for my kids. If my dad was verbally abusive to my siblings and me, I will be supportive and tell my kids that I love them every day. If my dad was interested in drinking and running around, then I will be the ultimate family man. If my dad missed little league games, then I will be at every activity my child has.

If my dad was never there for meals, then I will make sure to have breakfast with my child every morning."

These men decided that they wouldn't let genetics or their own dysfunctional family baggage prevent them from being good fathers. The risk, however, is that such men often put undue pressure on themselves to be the perfect dad. When they inevitably slip up or do something remotely similar to their own father, it crushes them. Veteran daddies recommend that you relax. Everyone screws up … on at least a semiregular basis.

Be Your Own Type of Dad

Every parent screws up from time to time no matter how hard they fight it. Veteran daddies recommend that you simply relax and don't worry about being like your father or anyone else. The great thing about being a parent is that you can be any type of father you want to be. You can wipe the slate clean and build your own fathering skills from the ground up. Of course we all have our own frame of reference and baggage we bring to any situation. But now is your opportunity to start fresh.

Think long and hard about what type of dad you want to become. Do you want to be the playful dad, the cool dad, the businesslike master of the house, the sensitive dad who listens, the affectionate father, or the disciplinarian? It is up to you. The great thing is that you don't have to be just one type. Just be your own type of dad.

I Don't Know Nuthin' 'Bout Birthin' No Babies, Miss Scarlet

One of the concerns guys have during pregnancy is that they will have to face their own ineptitude when it comes to babies. This is an area we know nothing about. Being a parent or father doesn't always come naturally, and it certainly doesn't come with directions or training. Veteran daddies say that they often felt unsure and fearful about whether they could physically take care of a child, but practicing ahead of time with friends' children helped. Even if they didn't have any practice, they rose to the occasion when their own child was born.

Picture the Traditions You Want to Establish

Shortly before Samantha was born, I remember going to buy bagels on a Saturday morning. I saw several fathers who were there with their children. Some of them appeared to be regulars and the children were of all ages. Some were on their way to soccer practice, others were watching their toddlers scurry around the store, and some were quietly reading the paper as their infant gently rested in the stroller.

Regardless of the activity, what struck me was that this seemed to be a regular event for many of them. As I watched these daddies interact with their kids, I couldn't help but picture myself with my child doing those same things, spending time one on one, bonding.

When Samantha was born, we borrowed from those dads at the bagel shop and began to have our own little Saturday morning "bagel date." Today it has evolved into "special daddy/daughter time," as she calls it. Bagels have given way to donuts, errands, and the weekly Home Depot trip, but the point is that we have something we both look forward to.

Think back to when you were a kid. Was there something special that you and your father did on a regular basis? Did he take you for a treat, or did you go with him to get a haircut or to get his shoes shined? Did you two go fishing on the weekends, or ride bikes together to get ice cream? Whatever the event, there may have been regular rituals or traditions that you two shared.

Creating your own traditions will ultimately mean a great deal to your child. They are a great opportunity for you and your baby to get to know one another. Remember that your wife already has developed a natural bond with the baby because she has been carrying it for nine months plus.

Daydreaming about these things is one of the special things that help prepare you for fatherhood and makes pregnancy seem to fly by. Think now about the traditions you want to start.

Before his son was born, Mark, an attorney in Austin, used to rise early on a Saturday morning and go to the IHOP to read the paper and talk with the old regulars over coffee. Six weeks after his son was born, Mark took his son with him not only to

show his buddies, but also to introduce his morning ritual to his son. Now every Saturday, Mark's little boy is right there by his side.

You Begin to Notice Every Child and Pregnant Woman

Before you learned that you were to become a father, you were probably oblivious to children except when they were acting up in public. But now that you are going to be part of the club, you've started to become aware of children. Everywhere you go you notice babies and women who are expecting. You notice fathers and children together. You notice babies while you are business trips, in restaurants, and at the park. You'll find yourself viewing children differently now that you know that you're becoming a father. A loud baby two rows behind you on the airplane was once annoying, but now you find yourself turning around in your seat to play peek-a-boo with that same baby. It is like your baby radar has been turned on and you are starting to look at the world through a parent's eyes.

What Will My Child Look Like?

Part of the fun of pregnancy is wondering who your child will look like. Obviously, you hope that the child looks something like you, not the deliveryman. When you daydream about playing with your child, you may even have a clear mental picture of what he or she will look like. You may hope that a boy will look like you and a girl will be pretty like her mother. You may hope for a mixture of each other's best features. You may secretly wish that your child doesn't get your big ears or your father-in-law's nose. You and your wife can wish and guess to your hearts' content, but the point is that you never know what the outcome of this genetic soup will look like.

When you finally meet your child, you may be pleasantly surprised … or not. Essentially, don't get your hopes set on what your child will look like. My wife and I were completely convinced that we would have dark-haired, dark-skinned children with my green eyes. We got a couple of fair-haired, fair-skinned kids with my wife's beautiful big dark eyes. You never know.

Do I Have Enough Love to Give?

Not to sound too deep or overly sensitive, but once you have your first child, you will learn how to love on a different level and begin to truly understand the idea of completely unconditional love. It can happen immediately or may hit you one day when your child is one or two years old, but you will wonder how you could possibly love anything more than you love your son or daughter.

Some dads wonder how they could possibly love a new child as much as they do their first baby. Veteran daddies say that they feared showing favoritism or even ignoring the new baby. If you already have a child, you may already feel pulled in so many directions with work, your relationship with your wife, your other child,

your home, and your friends that there is little time for yourself. How can you possibly find any more of yourself to give? I'm not going to kid you, it *is* tough, and sometimes one area of your life must be sacrificed, but you will manage and find enough love, time, and energy to give.

It is hard to explain, but you *will* love your second child just as much your first, though you will find that you love each child differently. You will love them equally, but you will love them and even play with them uniquely. It may not be apparent when your other child is born; it may take a couple of weeks or months for you to realize that your love as a parent has evolved.

My Kid Won't Act Like That

Part of envisioning your child is trying to picture how they will act and what kind of disciplinarian you will be. We all picture ourselves having only sweet, smart, and, most important, well-behaved kids. Like me, you may have been in a store or public place and seen a distraught parent futilely negotiating with a writhing, screaming two-year-old who you swear has 666 tattooed on his forehead. The embarrassed parent looks completely beaten as he finally picks the sweaty, sticky, screaming child up from the floor. As the parent leaves with the child, you look at your wife and say, "Honey, there is *no way* our kids will ever act like that."

Yeah, right. Every guy thinks that. I certainly did. I thought when a child threw a tantrum, it was certainly due to substandard parenting skills. Bear in mind this was before I actually had children. Word to the wise: hold off until you have some experience before you pass judgement on other parents. Parenting is like golf. It's harder than it looks.

I came to this realization when my daughter Samantha was two. I'd taken her with me to do some holiday shopping for my wife and we were at Victoria's Secret in the mall. I really don't feel altogether comfortable in this store during the holidays. It was wall-to-wall clueless men, and to make matters worse, I was there with a two-year-old and all her gear. Samantha decided it would be a good time to assert her independence. She crawled out of the stroller, lay down spread-eagle on the floor, and refused to get up. I pleaded like an idiot, but she wouldn't budge. I tried to remain calm and look cool as the attractive salesgirl asked if I needed help. When I tried to pick Samantha up from the floor, she screamed as though I were abusing her. I've never been so embarrassed in my life, and as I walked to the car with my sweaty, sticky daughter crying, kicking, and screaming, I remembered what I used to think about parents whose kids acted up—and I had to laugh.

Time to Get to Work

When women get pregnant, they become very aware of their health and alter their behavior accordingly. When many men learn that they are going to become a father, they become very aware of financial concerns and, consequently, of their career.

With a nine-month countdown until there is another mouth to feed, men often take stock of their own career and station in life. It is not uncommon for you either to take a look at your existing employment situation or to explore opportunities that will offer better pay, more flexibility, greater long-term opportunities, or less travel. Regardless of which you choose, you are likely to get more serious about your career in the time leading up to your child's birth.

This may manifest itself in your working harder and putting in longer hours. This can be a good strategy in the beginning, but veteran daddies agree that taking a long-term view of what will best serve you and your family is the smarter approach.

If your job requires you to travel, try to fit your schedule around the baby's due date. This may be easy if you have your own business, but if you work for someone else, it requires prior communication with your boss or manager. Share your concerns several months prior to the birth of your child; ask for an assignment that doesn't require travel during that time, or see if you can alter your schedule. More organizations are becoming aware of the stress that employees face trying to juggle family and business and are willing to work with them.

Taking Time Off

The Family Medical Leave Act has made it legally possible for employees, both male and female, to take time off to be with family during illness or upon the birth of a child. Your job will remain safe under the law. While all companies must adhere to this law, others go further by offering paternity leave, whereby a father may take off several days or weeks, similar to the maternity leave mothers often enjoyed.

The challenge is that while paternity leave is becoming a popular benefit, relatively few men are taking advantage of it. Some studies claim that less than 20 percent of men take advantage of the paternity leave available to them. There is still an unspoken rule that it is disadvantageous to your career. Sadly, in many organizations taking paternity leave labels you as someone who isn't serious about his career.

That is simply wrong. Men of all professions and across all social and economic levels are starting to understand that Dad is job one. Smart companies and managers are learning that loyalty is gained by helping people reach not only professional goals, but personal ones as well. And for many men, a significant personal goal is to spend more time with their family, to be there for the big events in their life.

You need look no further than professional golfer Phil Mickleson for an inspiring example of someone who puts family before career. Despite having a successful career, Mickelson had yet to win a major tournament. As Mickelson was going into the final round of the 1999 U.S. Open, battling for the lead with Payne Stewart and Tiger Woods. At home his wife was pregnant with their first child, who happened to be due the Sunday of the final round. The media asked Mickleson whether he would play through to possibly win his first major tournament or go home if his wife went into labor during the final round. For Mickelson, there was no question: he would be with his wife.

On the course during the final round, he was on the cell phone to his wife and had a chartered plane ready to whisk him away at a moment's notice. He was willing to walk away from a major championship. He was playing brilliantly as he, Stewart, and Woods battled neck-and-neck to the end. On the eighteenth hole, Stewart sank a putt to win.

Had Stewart not won, there would have been a play-off the next day, the day Mickelson's wife Amy delivered. He received much support from fans and professionals for his commitment to walk off the course and leave a championship. Yet others criticized him and said he should have considered remaining at the tournament. His response: "That disappoints me. As a father, there is nothing more important in life than raising that child."

- Regardless of whether your father is a positive or negative role model, use him as a road map to determine what type of father you do or don't want to become.
- Look at your own childhood to determine what strengths you want to adopt from your father and which characteristics you wish to avoid.
- Men often put undue pressure on themselves to be the perfect dad. When they inevitably slip up or do something remotely similar to their own father, it crushes them.
- Relax. Don't worry about being like your father or anyone else.
- Be your own type of dad. You can be any type of father you want to be. You can wipe the slate clean and build your own fathering skills from the ground up.
- Picture the traditions you want to establish with your child. Think back to your childhood memories; was there something special you did with your father on a regular basis?
- Don't worry. You have more than enough love to give. You *will* love your second child just as much as your first. You will love them equally, but differently.
- Plan your workload wisely. If your job requires you to travel, try to alter your schedule around the baby's due date.
- Plan to take at least a few days off after your child is born.

11

Getting the House Ready for Baby

As veteran daddies have pointed out, one of the ways you can feel more involved in the pregnancy and less like a spectator is to prepare the house for your newest roommate.

Women often go through a "nesting" phase late in the pregnancy, sometimes shortly before they go into labor. They anxiously clean, straighten, and prepare for baby. Men really aren't that different, but their nesting phase can occur at any point in the pregnancy. Here are a few things that you should do when you begin to prepare the roost.

Sit down with your wife to determine what needs to be accomplished and what she would like to see happen around the house before the baby arrives. Her ideas may be more decorative, such as painting a room or planting flowers, while your ideas may be more functional, such as putting up shelves, babyproofing, or cleaning out spaces. Regardless of what you do around the house, being active and doing simple home improvements can make you feel like a participant in the pregnancy. It provides a tangible contribution.

How Early Can We Prepare the Nursery?

You might decide to have everything cleared out and ready before baby's arrival, but this is a highly personal choice. Obviously, you want to be prepared and plan ahead, but some families hold to certain traditions, religious beliefs, or even superstitions that advise against too much preparation before baby is born. In some Jewish families, for example, it is considered bad luck to bring the crib and baby furniture into the house before the child is born. Some people wait to move the furniture in or even buy baby clothes until the child is born, not for religious reasons, but for practical ones.

Unfortunately, things don't always go smoothly with pregnancies and childbirth. There is always a risk of losing the baby at any point in the pregnancy and sometimes during the actual birth. I spoke with one veteran daddy and his wife who had prepared for their little girl's arrival very early. They had the nursery ready and the closet filled with little girl clothes. Sadly, in the sixth month, there were complications and the child was stillborn. Returning home to a nursery prepared for a little girl was an incredibly traumatic experience for both parents.

My wife was a little cautious about too much preparation for our first child. We prepared the room by having it painted. We purchased furniture, supplies, and clothes, but we did not want anything delivered until the baby arrived. The day that Samantha was born, we called the store and had them deliver everything to our home while we were still at the hospital. My mother-in-law and friends helped get everything ready for our arrival back home.

That "S" on My Chest Is for Safety Man

As your wife's due date approaches, you will find yourself taking life a little bit slower. You might stop at yellow lights rather than put the pedal to the metal. You might shout at people who speed through your neighborhood. You might start noticing small staples, nails, or debris on the floor that could harm a child. Your own protective paternal instinct is kicking in and you are concerned for the safety of your family. Not to say that you haven't been concerned up to this point, but your awareness hits a whole new level about halfway through the pregnancy.

Derrick, a reporter in San Francisco, says: "Around the sixth month, I started to have this irrational panic about my family's safety. I found myself calling the alarm company to upgrade our service. I went out and bought my wife new tires. Before that, I hadn't thought about her tires in years. I became afraid of flying for fear that we would crash and I would leave my child without a father."

Some guys become obsessed with reading *Consumer Reports* and knowing exactly what the safety ratings are for certain baby products, cars, and other household items. You will start to feel like a proud papa bear who is protecting his cubs.

There are several places to get the best information about products for baby and home. The *Consumer Reports* Web site, www.consumerreports.org, is one of the best resources to locate the safest products. On the Web, parenting sites such as www.babycenter.com and www.parentsoup.com have helpful reviews, write-ups, and chats to discuss certain products.

Babyproofing 101

We use the word "babyproof" to mean making the house safe for baby, but the truth is that real "babyproofing" doesn't need to happen until your child is about six to nine months old, when he becomes mobile. For the early part of his life, your baby will just lie there. Even when he learns to sit up, he still won't get into much trouble.

When he starts to crawl, however,

it is "Katy, bar the door." He will pull himself up on furniture, grab things from counters, stick his fingers into sockets, get in cabinets, open drawers, put things in his mouth, try to climb up stairs, and generally destroy anything in his path. But you have about six months after your child is born before you have to worry about that. In the meantime, here are a few things that you can do to babyproof a home so that it is suitable for an infant.

Clean the Carpets or Floors

When your child isn't in her cradle or bassinet or in your arms, she will likely be on a blanket or play mat on the floor. Several weeks before your wife is due, have the carpets professionally cleaned. Be sure to tell the service that a baby will be on the floor to make sure they use products that will be safe and won't leave a lingering residue.

Make an Open Space on the Floor

Again, since your baby will spend a lot of time on the floor, you might want to move some furniture to clear a wide space where you and baby can sit and play together. Make sure to leave plenty of room to move and walk around comfortably so no one risks falling near the baby.

Have Your Air Ducts and Filters Cleaned

Be sure to change all your air filters and have your ducts professionally cleaned. Your filters and air system can be full of dust and pollutants, which can be harmful to your baby's fragile lungs.

Change the Batteries in Smoke Detectors

Shortly before baby arrives is a particularly good time to make sure that all of your smoke detectors work properly and have fresh batteries.

Postpone Exterminator and Fertilizer Services

If you have exterminator, pest control, or fertilizer services visit regularly, you might consider skipping a few treatments while your wife is pregnant and shortly after the baby arrives. Many exterminators claim that the materials they use are safe, but there is no need to take any chances with fumes or toxins during this period.

Decide about Pets

Pets are like family members to many people. Up to this point in your life, your pet may have been like a child to you. But when a new baby arrives, you and your wife need to take a serious look at your pet's role in the family.

It doesn't matter whether you have a cat, a dog, or a pot-bellied pig, any pet may become jealous once the baby arrives. I realize that some breeds are excellent with children, but in the beginning, you should introduce the pet to the child slowly or choose to have the pet keep its distance at all times. If the pet shows the slightest bit of aggression toward the child, you should remove the pet from the house immediately.

Remove Any Chemicals That Can Produce Noxious Fumes

If you have chemicals, pesticides, cat litter, fertilizers, ant killers, or anything toxic or that can produce noxious fumes, you should remove them or keep them in a safe place where your wife and baby won't be exposed.

Think about Getting Rid of the Glass Table   We have friends whose house is a gorgeous contemporary showpiece. It looks like a museum. It is also about the most baby-unfriendly house I've been in: stark glass tables with sharp corners, tile and marble floors, spiral stairs, and sculptures and pottery on the floor. Your house and furnishings may be beautiful, but some items simply may not fit into your new lifestyle as parents. I'm not asking you to sell the home, but recognize what can pose a danger for a child and make at least one room baby-friendly, the others off limits.

If Babies Are So Small, Why Do They Have So Much Gear?

For someone so tiny, a baby sure needs a lot of things and takes up a lot of space. You may have to give up your home office, guest room, or junk storage room to make way for your baby and then fill it with expensive baby furniture, some of which you don't even understand.

Carl, a veteran daddy in Boston, says that when he was a baby, his parents didn't have a bassinet so they let him sleep in a drawer … open, I hope. Today they would risk being arrested.

If you are wondering what furniture and items you will need for your baby's nursery, or if you simply want to know what your wife has spent money on, here is a synopsis of baby gear and paraphernalia.

Changing Table   This looks like a credenza or dresser with a flat area to lay your baby on as you change her. It allows you to change the baby at a comfortable standing height. You will usually lay the baby on a cushion or soft pad on top of the table. There is a drawer or compartment for diapers, wipes, powders, clothes, blankets, or other things baby will need.

Crib, Cradle, or Bassinet?   If you are like most guys, you never knew that there was a difference between cribs, cradles, and bassinets. Essentially, they are all things that babies sleep in, but the differences are these:

A **crib** is a large stationary bed, usually with railings and slats on all sides. A child can sleep in a crib until she is two or three, or until she is large enough to sleep in a full-sized bed.

A **cradle** is like a smaller crib except that it has solid, not open or railed, sides and can rock or swing back and forth.

A **bassinet** is a small stationary bed that can be portable. Like a cradle, it does not have open or railed sides.

Both a bassinet and a cradle are used for the first two to four months. Parents often place cradles and bassinets in their own room for the first few weeks, until the baby is large enough to move to a permanent crib.

Glider   With a little marketing, these could easily replace barcaloungers and lazy boys. Gliders are simply the coolest rocking chair on earth. It rocks in a smooth, even motion that makes it easy for mom to feed the baby.

Swing   This device looks like two large upright triangles with a swing in the middle. It has a small battery- or spring-operated motor that keeps the swing rocking in a steady movement. You can strap your baby in and let the swing rock her to sleep. This can be a lifesaver in the middle of the night or when you have a crabby baby.

Bouncer   No, not a large man named Frankie stationed at your front door, but a small slinglike device that your baby can lie in at a forty-five degree angle. It is made of either metal or plastic and comes in either a large plastic unit like a car seat or a metal frame covered by fabric. The bouncer is great for when you don't want to lay the baby on the floor or in a crib, or for when you go to a restaurant and need a place to put the baby. You can place the bouncer on a table with you.

Car Seat   Children must *never* ride in the car unless they are in a car seat designed for the child's weight and size. Car seats come in a variety of shapes and styles. You can expect to spend around $100 for one, unless you use an all-in-one car seat/stroller, which can cost more. Be sure to check out the *Consumer Reports* Web site (www.consumerreports.org) for the latest findings on these and other baby

products. Until your child is around a year old or weighs thirty pounds, he should face backwards and always be placed in the back seat.

Stroller   Until humans develop multiple arms, there are times when you will need to put your baby down. Strollers allow your baby to rest or lie down while you push her around. Some strollers come as a multifunctional unit that doubles as stroller, baby carrier, and car seat. They come in all different styles, weights, materials, and prices. Be sure to get one that is lightweight, folds easily, and has several settings that allow your child to lie flat or ride sitting up.

Jogger Stroller   If you want to get back into shape and spend time with your child at the same time, then do yourself a favor and buy one of these. The three-wheeled jogger stroller looks like a racing stroller and in fact is made like a bicycle, complete with pneumatic tires and a hand brake. You won't be able to use this fully until your baby is a few months old, but then you can use it until your child is around four years old. Information can be found at *www.babyjogger.com*. My wife got one for me when our child was born, and it is one of my prized possessions. They aren't cheap, but they are certainly worth it.

High Chair   Babies can't sit up until they are six to nine months old, and even then they aren't stable. A high chair is an elevated chair with straps that allows you to feed your child easily. You really don't need to purchase a high chair until your baby is old enough to sit up. For the first few months, you will hold your baby in your arms to feed her.

Buy a Real Man's Diaper Bag   I know that you don't often hear "real man" and "diaper bag" used together, but consider this. When it is your turn to go solo with your child, you are going to be saddled with more baggage than some people take on a European vacation, including diapers, wipes, bibs, burp clothes, toys, blankets, change of clothes, and more. Where do they all go? In that cute little tote with the duck design, or the feminine floral bag your wife received at a shower? The bottom line is that you are likely to be stuck with a diaper bag that either looks like a purse or is simply too cute for words.

Believe me, you won't want to carry this. Go out and buy yourself a backpack that you use solely for baby's items, or purchase a nondescript diaper bag. Eddie Bauer makes a cool diaper bag that your buddies won't laugh at. It looks similar to one of their small duffel bags. It even comes with a side pocket for bottles and a changing mat. I've often made the mistake of forgetting my "manly" diaper bag and found myself carrying my wife's "fabulous" Nicole Miller bag with little baby bottles and storks on it, which can shake even the most confident man to his foundation.

DADDY SMARTS TOP TIPS on **GETTING THE HOUSE READY FOR BABY**

- **Make a checklist. Sit down with your wife to determine what needs to be accomplished before the baby arrives.**
- **Check out the following web sites for product and safety information: *Consumer Reports* (www.consumerreports.org); www.babycenter.com; www.parentsoup.com.**
- **You won't need to fully babyproof the house until your child is able to crawl. But in the meantime you can clean the carpets or floors, make an open space on the floor, have your air ducts and filters cleaned, change the batteries in smoke detectors, postpone the exterminator and fertilizer services, and remove any chemicals that can produce noxious fumes.**
- **Decide if your pet will remain indoors or be in contact with the baby.**
- **Consider getting rid of any glass tables or furniture that has sharp edges or may be unsafe for children.**
- **Buy a real man's diaper bag or backpack.**

PART 3

What Are My Wife and Baby Going Through?

Every morning, you look at your pregnant wife and witness incredible changes going on before your very eyes. You may have taken a health class in school, but just what is going on underneath the hood? This section discusses the changes in your wife's body and exactly what happens from the time you and your wife mix the genetic ingredients to create that bun in the oven until it is ready for delivery.

12

What's She Going Through?

This book focuses on what men are going through as they prepare to become fathers, but you also need to understand what your wife is going through, physically and emotionally, during this time. There are whole books devoted to this topic. If you want to learn more than is given here or just want more in-depth information about your wife and "what's under the hood," so to speak, I recommend that you check out a couple of "her" books, especially *What to Expect When You're Expecting*. This is a week-by-week guide for women and goes into the physiological changes that women experience during pregnancy in great detail. However, if you are a "give me the basics" kind of guy, the following is an overview of what your wife is experiencing.

First Trimester

A nine-month pregnancy is broken up into trimesters, each lasting three months. Each trimester is different for both your wife and the baby. During the first trimester (months 1–3), your wife is undergoing more internal changes to her body than at any other time throughout the pregnancy. While she may not *look* pregnant, this is when she experiences many of the common signs of early pregnancy, including morning sickness.

For about the first month to six weeks, there are not many signs of her condition. The most noticeable event is her missed period. Around six weeks after conception, she may start to develop early-pregnancy symptoms. These include sickness, nausea, fatigue, frequent urination, increased breast size, and soreness and increased sensitivity in her breasts.

What a Waist

During this time, generally around week eight, her uterus starts to expand, preparing to house your child for the next nine months. Normally, a woman's uterus is about the size of your fist. By the eighth week, it is about the size of a grapefruit and will continue to grow at an alarming rate. Your wife might also start to feel abdominal cramping. By the end of the first trimester, week twelve, it will be big enough to fill her pelvis. She will also begin to lose her waist. (This will piss her off to no end, so be prepared. You have been warned.)

By around week ten, you won't really notice her stomach getting larger yet, but her breasts will be noticeably bigger. Veteran daddies love this. Your wife is still normal-sized but with huge breasts. Thanks, God—good job. The catch is, they are probably so sore, plus your wife is in the bathroom every ten minutes to either pee or throw up, that this large breast phase comes and goes without your being able to take full advantage of the situation. Sorry.

Although your wife may not have any crazy menu requests, her nutrition is key. She needs to eat plenty of healthy foods and take her prenatal vitamins to keep up her strength and to make sure that the baby receives the proper nutrients while forming his or her organs and brain.

Why She Is Glowing

Another reason your wife needs to eat properly is that, in addition to her growing outwardly, she is growing internally. During pregnancy, a woman's blood flow volume increases by as much as 50 percent to accommodate the new baby. Pregnant women are said to have a healthy "glow" about them; this is one reason why. Because of the extra blood flow, your wife's hair will also grow faster

and thicker. It looks great now, but after pregnancy, when her blood flow goes back to normal, she will shed much of it. She won't go bald, but you may wonder if you have a new pet around the house.

Imagine That a Truck Carrying Hormones Had a Wreck

The first trimester and the early part of the second, your wife is at her moodiest. Her body is a walking chemistry set with hormones raging, and she is still getting used to it. Imagine enduring your wife's worst week of PMS … for four months. She is suffering from chemical imbalances as her body adjusts to its new visitor. Don't worry, it will even out—and if it doesn't, watch *SportsCenter*. Actually, if you have been around your wife when she has either gone on or off the Pill or her doctor has prescribed a different brand, you will understand what is going on. She is simply getting used to different hormone levels.

Second Trimester: Out of the Woods for Now

By the start of the second trimester, your wife is feeling much better. She has more energy and her morning sickness has likely subsided. While she is no longer nauseated, she may develop incredible heartburn and gas. She is also probably relieved because the chance of a miscarriage has dropped dramatically.

Do You Think Stretch Armstrong Has Marks on His Stomach?

Now is when many of the external

changes begin to happen. She will notice a dark line run from the top of her belly to the bottom. This is called the *linea nigra*. She is starting to gain weight, and her hips, waist, and stomach require that she start wearing loose clothing. She may begin to develop stretch marks. (Another thing she will be highly pissed about. You've been warned.) Women think they can prevent stretch marks on their stomach, hips, and breasts by rubbing lotions and creams on themselves. While you may enjoy helping her do this, the bad news is that it doesn't work. Stretch marks are genetically determined.

Around weeks fourteen to fifteen, your wife's breasts may begin to develop colostrum, an early form of breast milk. She may be able to squeeze some from her breasts. Around week nineteen or twenty, your wife's nipples may grow larger and darker. These changes are harmless and will subside after the child is born.

Also around this time, she will begin to take many of her prenatal tests, some of which measure for birth defects. If her doctor recommends that she have amniocentesis performed, which is common in women over 35, she will do so between the fifteenth and eighteenth weeks.

Oops—Excuse Me—Must Be the Gas

In the second trimester, she will start to feel the baby move inside of her. This starts as small flutters, called "the quickening." She may mistake it for gas at first. It will still be a few weeks before you can feel the baby from outside.

Your wife has probably gained five to ten pounds by the twentieth week. Her uterus has grown so large that it now reaches the top of her belly button. It will continue to grow in diameter at about a centimeter a week from here on. It is growing so quickly that as your wife's ligaments and muscles stretch to accommodate it, she will be very sore.

By the twentieth week, your wife will begin to feel tired and breathless. Her growing uterus has pushed her organs higher, putting pressure on her lungs. Because she is getting larger and her joints are beginning to loosen because of hormones, she may move more clumsily. She may also appear very forgetful. Some pregnant women claim that pregnancy kills brain cells. While this is debatable, pregnant women do have a lot to think about and may forget things, may seem preoccupied, or may not appear at the top of their game mentally. Late in the second trimester, her food cravings have also begun. You should start working out unless you want to look pregnant too, chubbo.

Third Trimester: She Is Ready for This to Be Over

At the start of the third trimester, weeks twenty-four to twenty-eight, your wife will find it difficult to sleep. She is uncomfortable and she may also suffer from nightmares. Bad dreams among pregnant women are fairly common. They worry about the health of the baby, if they will be good mothers, and their personal relationships. These fears manifest themselves in nightmares.

Your wife, because of increased size and bloodflow, will always feel hot. Your home may feel like a meat-locker. Turn down the AC and take a sweatshirt for yourself.

Your wife also needs to monitor her blood composition and blood pressure carefully. Pregnant women can easily become anemic—deficient in red blood cells—as well as suffer from preeclampsia, a form of high blood pressure.

By week twenty-eight, your wife's uterus is nearing her rib cage. She was already uncomfortable, but now she has leg cramps, varicose veins, and hemorrhoids to look forward to. (I bet you're thinking, "I'm glad men don't have babies.") Women gain around a pound a week during the third trimester. It is mind-boggling to watch your wife from one week to the next. She will start to see her doctor more frequently now, at least every other week, and then every week for the last month.

If you thought she had to pee a lot before, just wait. The baby seems to be dancing on her bladder and she will have to go to the bathroom all the time, or at least will have that sensation.

By the thirty-fourth or thirty-fifth week, your wife's feet, ankles, and hands will swell if they haven't already. She may also begin to feel tingling or numbness in her pelvis and legs. This is the baby applying pressure to her nerves. Your wife's uterus is underneath her rib cage, and she has gained at least twenty-five pounds.

Honey, I Dropped the Baby

At week thirty-seven, the baby is starting to drop into position for birth. You know by looking at a pregnant woman if the baby has dropped. She may have carried the baby near her ribs or the top of her stomach; now it looks like it is hovering around her pelvis. She can breathe much easier, although walking may be more of a challenge. Her cervix is starting to dilate and thin. The doctor may check internally to see how far the baby has dropped into the pelvis. At thirty-eight weeks, the baby is considered full term, and your wife can deliver at any time.

Throughout these changes, your wife will be happy, scared, unsure, and excited. Women have the additional burden of fearing not only for the safety of their child but for their own health. You can help by asking her questions and being there when she needs you.

- Pregnancy is broken up into trimesters, each lasting three months.
- While she may not look pregnant during the first trimester, she experiences many of the early signs of pregnancy, including morning sickness, nausea, fatigue, frequent urination, increased breast size, and soreness and increased sensitivity in her breasts.
- Your wife's nutrition is key in the first trimester. She needs to eat plenty of healthy foods and take her prenatal vitamins to keep up her strength and to make sure that the baby receives the proper nutrients while forming its organs and brain.
- By the start of the second trimester, your wife is feeling much better. She has more energy and her sickness has likely subsided. While she is no longer nauseated, she may develop incredible heartburn and gas. She is no doubt relieved because the chance of a miscarriage has dropped dramatically.
- If her doctor recommends that she have amniocentesis performed, which is common in women over 35, she will do so between the fifteenth and eighteenth weeks.
- By the twentieth week, your wife will begin to feel tired and breathless. Her growing uterus has pushed her organs higher, putting pressure on her lungs. Because she is getting larger and her joints are beginning to loosen due to hormones, she may move more clumsily. She may also appear very forgetful.
- At the start of the third trimester (weeks twenty-four to twenty-eight), your wife will find it difficult to sleep. She may worry about the health of the baby, her parenting skills, and her personal relationships. These fears manifest themselves in nightmares.
- Your wife, because of increased size and blood flow, will always feel hot. Your home may feel like a meat-locker.
- At week thirty-seven, the baby starts to drop into position for birth. She may have carried the baby near her ribs or the top of her stomach, but now it appears to be hovering around her pelvis.
- At thirty-eight weeks, the baby is considered full term, and your wife may deliver at any time.

13

How Is My Baby Developing?

Ah, the miracle of life. You may have taken eighth-grade health class and know that the sperm and the egg collide, cells divide, and nine months later we have a little human, but here is a crash course on what happens in between.

First Trimester: Divide and Conquer

After you and your wife have sex and your sperm fertilizes the egg, the egg implants itself into the lining of the uterus. The egg will eventually split in two; one half will become your child while the other half will become the placenta, which sustains your child during his journey. Amniotic fluid will form as well. This will fill the uterus and help cushion the baby.

The first trimester is a fast and furious time in your baby's development. As early as week five, the embryo is about the size of an apple seed, and a basic placenta and umbilical cord are functioning to provide nourishment and oxygen. By week six, your baby's heart has developed and is beating, although it is only about the size of a poppy seed. His major organs such as the kidneys are starting to develop. It'll be a while before he's ready to play in the NBA, however, because he is still about a quarter of an inch long and looks more like a tadpole than a baby.

By week seven, he is the size of a pinto bean. His head is oversized and he has dark spots where his eyes will form. Small buds, which look like paddles, represent his arms and legs. He is still an embryo, and has a small tail that will disappear in the next few weeks. By week eight, your baby's heart has developed chambers and his brain is growing more complex. His arms are no longer buds and can bend at the elbows. By week nine, the baby is considered a fetus.

Your child weighs barely one ounce, but he will gain weight quickly from this point on. His basic cell structure is in place, as are all of his organs including genitals, eyes, legs, and arms, although they are not yet fully developed. Toward the end of the first trimester, your baby is between 1.75 and 2.5 inches long. His length will double over the next three weeks. Smaller details are starting to develop, such as fingernails and hair.

Second Trimester: Everything Is in Place

At the beginning of the second trimester, your child is beginning to look more human. His eyes started out on either side of his head, like a fish's, but they now face forward. He is three to four inches long and weighs about an ounce. Despite his tiny size, the baby looks completely formed.

Over the next few weeks, the baby's weight triples and he develops *lanugo,* a fine hair all over his body. Don't worry, it falls out after he is born. He will also start to hiccup, which is preparing him for breathing. If you could see him, he fits into your hand and weighs almost five ounces. He is about as big as a peach.

By week seventeen, his systems are all working, including his circulatory system. He is even inhaling and exhaling amniotic fluid to strengthen his lungs for birth. His bones, which have been flexible cartilage to this point, are starting to harden. It is dur-ing this time that many people choose to have an ultrasound. If you do, you might find your baby moving, sucking his thumb, or kicking. This is the time you may find out that he is a she.

She Keeps Growing and Growing

At week twenty, about the halfway mark, your baby is 6.5 inches long and weighs about nine ounces. Her brain is developing specialized areas such as those that control smell, taste, and vision. She is also developing a waxy white coating called *vernix caseosa,* which protects her from being submerged in amniotic fluid for so long. It wipes off at birth.

At twenty-two weeks, your child can hear noises outside of the womb, such as music and your voice. Many parents start talking to their children at this point, reading or playing music. During the next few weeks, over the second trimester, your baby's main development will be in size. She is gaining weight and growing in length. Again, much of the primary development was formed in the first trimester.

Third Trimester: In the Clear

At twenty-eight weeks, your child has reached a milestone: she could survive if born prematurely. Her lungs, while immature, are capable of working. She is probably between twelve and fifteen inches long and weighs between two and three pounds. She can also open her eyes.

By the thirty-second week, she is not moving much, simply because she is running out of room. She may be close to eighteen or nineteen inches long. She will gain half of her birth weight in the next seven weeks.

At week thirty-five, your baby's

lungs are fully developed. Respiratory problems were once a major killer of infants born before term, but because of technological advances, 99 percent of babies born at this point survive. She is starting to shed her vernix caseosa and lanugo, which will remain in the amniotic fluid. Your baby may swallow some of this, which will result in her first poop after birth, which is called meconium.

At week thirty-seven, your baby begins to drop into position for birth. Her head will rotate and she will start to move into the pelvis. From this point on, she will gain weight faster than she will grow in length. She is mostly adding fat layers. (Hey, aren't we all?)

Hey, Daddy, Come and Get Me

At week thirty-eight, your baby is considered full term and can come any day from here on through week forty-two. Only 5 percent of babies are born on their due date. It is not uncommon for your baby to be anywhere from two weeks early to two weeks late. Doctors do not let women go past forty-two weeks without inducing labor or performing a C-section.

From this point forward, the bun is in the oven and the timer is about to go off. Your baby is ready for delivery.

DADDY SMARTS TOP TIPS **on HOW THE BABY IS DEVELOPING**

- By week six, your baby's heart has developed and is already beating. His major organs, such as kidneys, are starting to develop. He looks more like a tadpole than a baby.
- By week nine, the baby is considered a fetus.
- Toward the end of the first trimester, your baby is between 1.75 and 2.5 inches long. His length will double over the next three weeks. Smaller details are forming, such as fingernails and hair. His genitals are beginning to show and develop as well.
- At the beginning of the second trimester, your child is beginning to look more human. He is about three to four inches long and weighs about an ounce. Despite his tiny size, the baby looks completely formed.
- By week seventeen, all his systems are working, including his circulatory system. He is even inhaling and exhaling amniotic fluid to strengthen his lungs for birth. It is during this time that many people choose to have an ultrasound.
- At twenty-two weeks, your child can hear noises outside the womb, including your voice.
- At twenty-eight weeks, your child has reached a milestone: she could survive if born prematurely. Your baby's lungs, while immature, are capable of working. She is probably between twelve and fifteen inches long and weighs between two and three pounds. She can also open her eyes.

- At week thirty-five, your baby's lungs are fully developed. Ninety-nine percent of babies born at this point survive.

- At week thirty-seven, your baby is beginning to drop into position for birth. She may be close to eighteen or nineteen inches long. She will gain half of her birth weight in the next seven weeks.

- At week thirty-eight, your baby is considered full term and can come any day from here on through week forty-two. Only 5 percent of babies are born on their due date. It is not uncommon for your baby to be anywhere from two weeks early to two weeks late.

14

Hospital FAQ (Frequently Asked Questions)

Unless you are planning on having your baby at home, you need to choose and check out a hospital. Many hospitals advertise their state-of-the-art birthing centers, how they cater specifically to women, or other great marketing claims, but where you deliver your baby is limited to where your wife's doctor has operating privileges and what your insurance plan covers.

Some doctors are able to deliver at several hospitals. If this is the case and your insurance will cover it, you have a few choices to make. Veteran mommies and daddies suggest that if you and your wife are deciding between hospitals, you tour each one.

You should try to make your hospital tour sometime early in the last trimester. Generally, your wife's doctor will give her information about setting up a hospital tour, including whom to contact. Such tours are free and are given privately or in groups, depending on the hospital. When

selecting a hospital, some things that you should consider are:

Doctor's Preference

Ask your wife's doctor at which hospital he prefers to work. The doctor is familiar with the facilities and staff of the different hospitals and may be more comfortable with one hospital over another. Don't forget that doctors have reputations at each hospital and it would help to be at a hospital where your doctor has influence.

Location

How far is the hospital from your house? You don't want to drive across town and risk delivering your child in the back of your car. However, the closest hospital may not be the best facility.

Reputation

Ask around. Find out if any of your friends or coworkers have delivered at a particular hospital and if so, what their experience was. Word of mouth counts for a lot. However, don't put too much weight on only one negative opinion. If you hear several negative comments or you begin to see a pattern, then you might wonder if that hospital is the right choice for you.

Facilities

Is the hospital undergoing construction, and if so, will it be completed by the time your wife is due? If construction will be going on, then make sure you know where you need to go when then big day arrives. There may be detours.

Do the facilities appear modern, clean, and in good condition? Are the labor and delivery rooms in good condition, or do they look as though half the population of your city has already delivered there?

Don't Get Too Attached to the Cool Birthing Room on the Tour

I guarantee you that while on the tour your wife will see a state-of-the-art birthing room, complete with cute décor, pictures on the wall, VCR, and stereo to pipe in New Age music as your child enters the world, and she will think: "This is where I want my child to be born." She will look at you and say, "Honey, I hope we get one of these rooms."

Every hospital shows these rooms to expectant parents, but they fail to tell you that they have only a few of them. Unfortunately, there is no guarantee that you will get one, because on the day your child is born, every woman in town will be delivering at that same hospital. However, you can always deliver your child in a wonderful spare closet that looks like an ordinary, drab, cold hospital room. Talk about bait and switch. If your wife has her heart set on being in one of these wonder rooms, then make sure that your hospital has a bunch of them, not just three or four. And try to prepare your wife for the very real possibility of not being in one of them.

Staff

Does the staff appear friendly, or are they indifferent when you ask questions? What is the reputation of the staff? What do your friends and coworkers who have given birth here say?

Parking

Is the parking free for dads? Many hospitals give father's tokens for parking or have special spots for parents. Find out where you are supposed to park when you and your wife come for the big event.

Security

Throughout the country there have been cases where infants have been abducted from hospitals or babies have been accidentally switched. While these certainly aren't regular occurrences or something that you should dwell on, you should ask the hospital staff some questions about security.

See the nursery and ask what the procedures are for visitors and checking the child out of the nursery. Inquire about security bracelets, passwords, and cameras. These should be considered minimum safety requirements. Every facility is different, so check it out.

Financial Considerations

During your visit, ask to speak with someone in the accounting department who can answer questions about payment plans, insurance, and even credit cards.

Once you have chosen to deliver at a particular hospital, some facilities will give you and your wife paperwork so you can complete the registration process ahead of time. If you're given such papers, complete them and turn them in promptly. Also make sure to locate where you need to go when you register. This will save you time and make things go more smoothly on Labor Day.

Back to School: Lamaze and Childbirth Class

Picture for a moment that you and your wife are in a tender moment in a dark room. You are seated on the floor holding your wife from behind and you're gently caressing and massaging her. Her breathing becomes harder as you offer soft words of encouragement, like "C'mon, baby. That's it. You're almost there." Sounds pretty exciting, huh?

Now picture eight other pregnant couples in the same room with you as an instructor is counting off, "One, two, three. Okay, you're having a contraction." I don't know what *you* were thinking about, but I was describing childbirth class.

Your wife may have read a library-ful of pregnancy and childbirth books

in order to prepare for delivering a baby. And she's not alone. You have jumped on the pregnancy bandwagon yourself by reading this book. But regardless of how much you've read, some couples feel like they still have more to learn. They want the reassurance of knowing exactly what labor and delivery will be like. And that's okay. It is perfectly normal for rookie moms and dads to want to know exactly what to expect.

For your wife, however, it goes beyond the fear of the unexpected. There is an additional concern: pain. She has heard the horror stories of how painful contractions can be and she wants to know how to deal with them. Dads want to know more about the technical aspects of childbirth. To learn these things, many couples attend birthing classes.

It's Not Lamaze Class

Childbirth classes, often mistakenly called Lamaze classes, are frequently given by hospitals, midwives, and other birthing professionals. Lamaze is actually a breathing technique that women can use to manage pain during labor.

You and your wife can attend these classes at any time, but it is most common for couples to take them late in the second trimester or early in the third. Veteran couples recommend that you don't wait till too late in the pregnancy to start classes, because if the baby arrives early you may not have completed all of your classes. You can take classes that meet several times over a few weeks and others that try to cram everything into one or two classes.

Your wife's doctor will provide her with information about types of classes, pricing, location, and scheduling. Some classes are very in-depth and cover all elements of pregnancy, from nutrition and general health through birth and baby care; others are more of a crash course in pregnancy, labor, and delivery.

These classes can be helpful, but are not required. Naturally, it is mostly rookie couples who attend. Once they have gone through an actual childbirth, many couples don't feel the need to take the class again, unless it has been several years between children.

VBAC Is Not a Sport Utility Vehicle

One interesting group of veteran parents you will find in childbirth class are women who are planning to have a VBAC delivery. VBAC stands for Vaginal Birth After Cesarean. If a woman has previously given birth but the baby was born via C-section, there is a chance that she has not experienced the full range of labor. In many ways, the vaginal birth of this child will be just as if she is having a child for the first time.

Many veteran daddies have felt that the classes were somewhat helpful to them, but it was their wives who received the most benefit. Birthing classes are educational, but more from a technical perspective, helping you understand what actually happens during labor. You will probably see a video of an actual birth, which will completely disgust you. Ours looked like some bad Swedish home movie. What was most helpful for me was the doll that they used to show how the baby moves through the birth canal and emerges at birth.

Who Teaches These Classes?

They are often given by nurses or by midwives. A midwife is a person who is not a doctor but is specially trained in coaching women through labor and delivery, often a registered nurse. In certain states, midwives often do the actual delivery of babies, particularly in home births. However, since they are not doctors, they are not qualified or equipped to handle certain serious complications that may arise during birth. There are some states in which midwives are not licensed to deliver babies.

Some couples swear by midwives. Your wife may have already chosen whether she wishes to use one. Their primary job is to make a woman more comfortable and to ease her delivery.

Regardless of their profession, childbirth teachers are often birthing veterans in the sense that they are either moms or have helped deliver many babies. Speaking of veterans, our instructor had given birth to eight children, now between the ages of three and twenty-three. Needless to say, we listened to what she said.

Does the Breathing Technique Really Work?

Lamaze is the breathing technique taught in many of these birthing classes. It is intended to help a woman focus on something other than the pain of labor. It also allows the husband to participate by helping his wife concentrate on her breathing and visualization.

The truth is that it works for some couples. Others think it is a complete waste of time. There is a lot going on during labor, and remembering to do the breathing is half the battle. But we found that it worked well as a concentration aid. When it came time, my wife did not want me to talk or count out loud as we were taught in class. She simply wanted me to hold up my fingers so she could focus on something.

Your wife may find something else that works for her. Specific techniques are taught, but ultimately, the only right thing is whatever keeps your wife's mind off the pain. Every woman is different, so don't put undue pressure on yourself or your wife to win the Lamaze gold medal.

That first morning of class was almost surreal as I watched eight plump women simultaneously waddle in with clueless pillow-toting husbands in tow. Until birthing class, I had never seen so many pregnant women at once in my life. It was nice, however, to finally be surrounded by guys who were going through the exact thing that I was.

Your wife will instantly bond with the other women in the class, sharing intimate details of bodily functions and other goings-on as if they were long lost friends. The guys who are there are friendly but won't seem as eager to open up with each other. You should take advantage of this opportunity to be around other dads. Whether you have much in common socially, economically, or otherwise, this may actually be your only exposure to other dads who are currently going through what you are.

Also, if you and your wife seem to click with another couple in your class, make it a point to stay in contact with them. You might try to get together for dinner or a prebaby movie. It may be a while after the baby arrives before you get to do such things again. You might even try to stay in touch after your children are born. It would be fun to have someone who knows just what you are going through and with whom you can compare notes.

Take One for the Team

I guarantee that at some point, generally during the breathing exercises, you are going to feel like the biggest dork in the world. Looking around and seeing eight other men massaging their rotund wives won't make you feel any more secure. You will be waiting for someone to jump out and say, "Smile, you're on *Candid Camera!*"

Inevitably, there will be one couple who takes it too seriously. These teacher's pets ask all the stupid questions and practice their breathing technique so realistically that you will think she is going to pop that baby out right there in class.

While some daddies benefit from the classes, others think that they are pointless and about as bad as going shopping for maternity clothes. If you do, it's okay. However, the key is to keep it to yourself and take one for the team. Your wife may find the classes incredibly valuable.

And even if she doesn't get much information from them, being around other pregnant women will reassure her and make her feel more comfortable, even normal. Don't make too much fun of the classes or the people in them ... at least, not to your wife. And whatever you do, don't let her go alone.

DADDY SMARTS TOP TIPS on **HOSPITAL FAQ**

- Make your hospital tour sometime early in the last trimester.
- When selecting a hospital, consider doctor's preference, location, reputation, and facilities.
- During your hospital visit, does the staff appear friendly or are they indifferent when you ask questions? What is the reputation of the staff? What do your friends and coworkers who have given birth here say?
- Find out where you are supposed to park when you and your wife come for the big event. See if they offer parking tokens for fathers and family.
- Visit the nursery and ask about the procedures for visitors and for checking the child out of the nursery. Inquire about security bracelets, passwords, and cameras.

- During your visit, ask to speak with someone in the accounting department who can answer questions about payment plans, insurance, and credit cards.
- Complete any registration and paperwork ahead of time. This will save you a lot of time and make things go more smoothly on Labor Day.
- Take advantage of birth class as opportunity to be around other dads.
- Don't make fun of the classes no matter how corny you think they are.

The Great Debates

In creating a family, you and your wife will bring strong opinions and feelings to the table as you determine such things as a name for your child, day care, and how you will raise your kids.

For every couple, these and other issues become the focus of great debates and heated conversations.

These are also known by their more common name ... "fights."

15

Boy versus Girl

Throughout the entire pregnancy, friends, family, coworkers, and strangers standing in the grocery store checkout line will inquire, "What are you having?" After this happens for what seems to be the millionth time, your impulse is to say "Uh, a *baby*?" but you smile and proudly say that you're having a boy or a girl. Unfortunately, if you don't know the sex of your child, then you're asked the follow-up question: "So, do you want a little boy or a little girl?" What is the right answer?

That's What Everyone Says

Well, allow me to share with you the generic, one-size-fits-all, politically correct answer to this question that every expectant parent uses. Learn it well, because you will say it at least five times a day. Repeat after me: "It doesn't matter, I just want a healthy baby."

Sure, everyone wants a healthy baby, but c'mon, you must have a preference, right? The truth is that despite our efforts to avoid any type of favoritism, we all secretly (or not so secretly) lobby for a specific sex. But before you begin to cheer for a prince or princess, an outboard or inboard, a colt or filly, or any of the other euphemisms often found on the bathroom doors of finer truck stops everywhere, you and your wife need to decide whether or not you even want to find out the gender of your child.

Every couple asks themselves, "Should we learn the sex of our child?" Psst—do you want to know? I've done it both ways. I've treasured the buildup and excitement. But I've also been surprised, and veteran daddies agree that there is something special about running out of that delivery room and shouting to your family and friends, "It's a [*insert gender of choice*]!"

And the Envelope, Please

With our first child, my wife and I initially chose not to find out. Now, realize that in this decision, we were each reacting completely opposite to our usual personalities. I love surprises and suspense. My wife, however, requires a detailed schedule that we shall not deviate from. Surprises are not found on the agenda and they will not be included or tolerated. But when it came to our children, Meredith announced that she wanted to be surprised. I was shocked. She argued, "This is one of life's truly great surprises, and I want to experience it." This was coming from the woman who plans our weekends four months out.

On the other hand, the suspense was killing me. I wanted to know so I could get on with thinking about life with a son or a daughter. I have a hard enough time thinking about two things at once, so trying to visualize for both a boy and a girl was impossible. I also wanted to know so we could pick a name and stop referring to the child in my wife's tummy as "it," "baby," or "little bean." I wanted to really connect with my child. I also wanted to start buying gender-appropriate gear. I had already purchased a little basketball, which could be used whether we had a boy or a girl.

In our situation, like that of many other couples, there was discussion, pleading, debate, and cajoling. I ultimately decided to go with my wife on this one. This is another situation where you and your wife must be in complete agreement. The suspense can, according to veteran mommies and daddies, be one of the most satisfying parts of the pregnancy. So if one person feels strongly about not knowing the sex, pushing the issue can rob them of that experience. Guys, if you

are dying to find out and she is reluctant, don't force it. Wait a few months. It is exciting regardless of whether you learn the gender of your child in a doctor's office or in the delivery room.

If you and your wife cannot agree and can't come to a decision on whether or not to discover the baby's sex, then make a pact in blood that the parent who learns the baby's sex will not tell the other one, hint around, buy a certain color, purchase gender-specific toys, or tell anyone else who could possibly spill the beans. It is tough to keep this secret for several months, and if you screw up, even a little, you are cheating the other parent of their experience. Do this and you can certainly expect fights, tears, and sleeping alone. Veteran daddies don't recommend one person knowing and the other not, but it's your call.

I can't count the number of couples who have shed tears because some bonehead sonogram tech slipped up and mentioned the sex of the baby. If this occurs, remember, it was an accident. Okay, it's a really *big* accident, but it was not done intentionally to rob you or your wife of an experience.

■

Ken, a salesman in Phoenix, says that when the sonogram tech accidentally referred to the child as "he," his wife freaked out. The tech tried to backpedal, saying that she called all the babies "he," but Ken's wife didn't buy it and was crushed. She went into

hysterics and called the doctor, saying that this woman had ruined her pregnancy and she wanted the technician fired. (I'll bet your wife is looking pretty tame compared to this.) The doctor finally calmed her down, but she was bitter about having the surprise ruined. Accidentally revealing the sex of an unborn child is not a fireable offense, but tell that to Ken's wife.

Hello, My Name Is … Don't Tell Me

Some sonogram techs will ask you ahead of time if you want to know the baby's sex. Otherwise, it is your responsibility to stop them from saying anything. Some sonogram techs will tell you before they start that they refer to all babies as "she," which does not refer to your child's sex. Others will tell you that they refer to the child simply as "baby."

Samuel, a veteran daddy in Boston, recommends that you and your wife go to an office supply store and purchase those big generic name tags with the blank space for you to fill in the name. In the space where the name is supposed to go, write in big letters, "DON'T TELL US!"

What If the Surprise Is Blown?

Don't seethe with bitterness like Ken's wife if the surprise is blown. You still have a healthy little child, so refocus your energy on something positive. Now you know and can choose names and clothes. You can settle on colors for the nursery and finally have people stop asking you whether you want a boy or a girl.

As I mentioned earlier, with our first child we originally chose not to learn the sex. However, my wife required amniocentesis. However small the chance of Down's syndrome, as rookie parents we were nervous, scared, and just plain freaked. I was much more freaked than my wife, but we both were on edge, to say the least.

It was the week before Thanksgiving, and we knew we would have to wait two weeks for the test results to come back. We didn't want to spend the holiday with *that* hanging over our family, so Meredith and I decided that we would change our original plans and find out the baby's sex at this time. (An ultrasound/sonogram is performed to guide procedure, aiding the doctor as he inserts the needle. Because the ultrasound allows you to see the child, you can learn the sex if you choose.)

We made this choice because we wanted to focus on something exciting and positive for those two weeks rather than spend time thinking about a possible negative outcome. It was a smart thing. Fortunately, the tests were fine, but discovering that we were to have a little girl took our minds off anything else and lifted our spirits.

What Will I Do with a Little [*Insert Gender*]?

First of all, it is perfectly normal to favor one gender over the other. Everyone does, just a little bit. The key is not to go overboard in your enthusiasm for one sex over the other.

In some cases, a preference doesn't mean that you necessarily *want* one gender over another as much as you *fear* having one gender over another. There are some men, for instance, who fear having a little girl. They claim this is because they won't know how to deal with a little girl. "What do they do?" "How do they play?" "I know how to handle a boy, but a girl?" Or it may be the other way around. For a long time, I was fearful of having a boy.

My father was not very active with me growing up and when he was, he tended to be rather dictatorial, as was common with many fathers of that generation. I did not have a brother or close uncle as I grew up. My closest relationships were with my mom, my sister, and other women in my family.

When it came time for me to have children, I was a bit reticent about having a boy. I feared that I would fall into the same trap as my father and would be very hard on him. I was fearful of not knowing how to express myself toward a son. As it turned out, my second child was a boy and I quickly overcame my irrational fears because I realized that I could be whatever kind of dad I wanted to be.

I'm here to tell you that caring for a boy or a girl is really not that different, outside of some basic hygiene issues. And as far as how they play, you don't have to worry about that for quite some time. Your baby boy or girl will likely lie there, eat, sleep, and

cry for several months. And that doesn't depend on whether it's a boy or a girl.

I'll Take the Boy and the Points

There are plenty of old wives' tales about how to determine the sex of a baby beforehand. People will inspect an expectant mother like a piece of fruit to determine if she is carrying high or low. Others claim to know the sex according to whether your wife craves or disdains certain foods. Some will even analyze the color of her hair to tell whether is a boy or a girl. Your buddies may have big money riding on an office pool to determine if you will have a Buck Jr. or a Li'l Sissie. It is all meant in fun, but can grow wearisome toward the end.

You and your wife may have your own ideas about the sex of your child. You may feel that you have some psychic power that allows you to see the baby's sex and you're convinced it is a boy. You refer to the baby as "he." You don't even choose girls' names because you're 100 percent sure that it's a boy. Veteran daddies recommend that you try to contain your enthusiasm. It is great to be excited, and you can lobby, root, hope, and pray for either a boy or a girl, but unless you've had an amnio or ultrasound performed and know the results, nothing is certain.

Another reason to keep your enthusiasm on an even keel is for your wife's sake. If you go overboard in your desire for a certain sex and then don't get it, she may wonder if you will love that child as much or be disappointed. Remember that she already has an irrational fear that you will leave and she will be left alone. Don't set yourself up for disappointment in the delivery room.

Hey, My Son Is Missing Some Equipment

If when the big day arrives you find that your little baby "boy" is missing some equipment and is wrapped in a pink blanket, you probably won't even care. But in the rare event that you are disappointed, you had better bite your tongue, put on a happy face, and look in your child's eyes. Within five minutes of staring at that little face, that reflection of you, you will wonder how in the world you could have possibly wanted anything but what you were blessed with.

DADDY SMARTS TOP TIPS on **BOY VERSUS GIRL**

- If one person feels strongly about not knowing the sex, pushing the issue can rob them of that experience.
- Some sonogram techs will ask you ahead of time if you want to know the baby's sex. Otherwise, it is your responsibility to stop them from saying anything.
- It is perfectly normal to favor one gender over the other.

- Caring for a boy or a girl is really not that different, outside of some basic hygiene issues. For the first few months, all babies do the same things anyway.
- It is great to be excited, and you can lobby, root, hope, and pray for a boy or a girl, but unless you have had a test performed and know the results, nothing is certain.
- Keep your enthusiasm on an even keel for your wife's sake. If you go overboard in your desire for a certain sex and then don't get it, she may wonder if you will love that child as much.

16

Choosing A Name

For some couples, agreeing on a suitable name can be as tricky as negotiating a Middle East peace agreement. Every couple has this debate. Do we go with family names, trendy names, or biblical names? Do we honor someone we know or do we name our child after our favorite centerfielder? Do we want a funky spelling? Do we make up a name?

Some people have had names passed down for generations, while others select names from the movie screen. One successful Dallas restaurateur is rumored to have named his child Liberty, after the movie *The Man Who Shot Liberty Valance*. Everyone has his or her own way of selecting names and all of them are valid. There is no right or wrong way to select a name.

If Only We Had a Family Member in a Biblical Soap Opera

My wife and I went through an agonizing debate naming both of our children. As much as my wife and I

see eye to eye, can finish each other's sentences, and generally complement one another, when it came to what to name our children, we reached an impasse. But unless we wanted our baby to go through life as "hey, you" we had to come up with a name, like it or not.

She is from the old school and favors strong Biblical (boring) names. I, on the other hand, would have no problem naming a child Storm, Steele, Ridge, or any other name generally found on daytime soaps. We considered family names, but the problem was that I have a grandmother named Thetis— 'nuff said. Eventually, we finally settled on Samantha and Skylar. Personally, I think I persuaded her to come over to *my* side.

As you and your wife are choosing names, it is your duty as a rookie dad to make sure that the names selected meet very stringent testing requirements. Following are a few of the tests that you should put each name through.

The Nickname Test

Richard equals Dick. Need I say more?

The Playground Test

Will your child's name hold up on the playground? The benchmark here is Nick. Nick's your buddy. Nick's your pal. Nicky's from the old neighborhood. The girls all love Nicky. Nick is good. Please do *not* saddle your kid with a name that destines him to a childhood of teasing and playground beatings by kids named Chuck. Examples here include Clarence, Tad, and Ira.

The Exotic Dancer Test

In your best cheesy announcer voice, say, "Introducing on the left stage, it's [*insert daughter's name*], Brandi, Electra, Bambi, and Barbie!" If that sentence flows a little too easily, you should seriously reconsider the name you've chosen. C'mon, guys, we all like stripper names when we're single, but it's a little different when it's your daughter.

The Alternative Meanings Test

Does the name you're considering have an alternate use or definition you are unfamiliar with? The buddy of one veteran daddy was going to name his child Simeon ("simian," meaning ape-like) if it was a boy. Fortunately, he had a girl. Being a little boy named after a character on the *Planet of the Apes* is not a good way to go through life.

The Names That No One Can Possibly Live Up To Test

Kids have a tough enough time growing up without carrying the extra weight of being named Jesus, Zeus, Apollo, Moses, Duke, Madonna, Venus, or Rocky. Inevitably, Rocky will grow up to be a fabulous 5'5" red-haired interior decorator.

Justin, a big fan of the Tom Selleck show *Magnum PI*, named his son Magnum. The only problem is that it looks like genetics might be working against the boy. With a name like Magnum, you would hope he'd grow up to be about 6'4", but poor Magnum's mom is 5'2" and his dad might hit 5'7" on a good day.

The Self-Fulfilling Prophecy Test

If a name helps to shape a child's self-image, why on earth would you name him Bubba?

The Ex-Girlfriend's Name Test

Don't even try it.

The Ex-Boyfriend's Name Test

You're granted automatic veto power.

The Bad Memory Test

We develop opinions about certain names based on people we have known in the past. There will be names that one of you loves but for some reason the other will have a bad memory that involves someone with that particular name. Tom, a veteran daddy in Chicago, says, "My wife loved the name Taylor for a boy, but I knew a Taylor in college who I couldn't stand. Forget it." Disliking a name under the "bad memory" test needs no logic to be valid and has no expiration date. Your wife may have been teased by a Karen in third grade, so you can count on it that you will never have a child named Karen.

Foreign Names

I'm all for a little international flair. But unless you are originally from the country where the name originated, think long and hard before giving your child a name that, while very common in, say Luxembourg or Tonga, needs constant explanation here in the old USA. One little boy in my daughter's day care was named, I kid you not, Espn (pronounced Espin). His native Texan mom said it was a popular Danish name. Yeah, Danish for sports.

Also, make sure that a foreign name works well with your last name. Javier Greenblatt or Anka O'Brian sound like bars in Cancun. I loved the name Paolo, but Paolo Richardson didn't quite roll off the tongue. It got the ax.

My Name Is Michael—Not Mike or Mikey

Some people will automatically try to shorten proper names that you have given to your child. You may not mind, but parents often feel very strongly about the name they gave to their child and do not wish it to be altered or abbreviated. If your daughter is named Gabrielle and you want her to be known that way, you need to gently correct people from the beginning. Be kind but firm about how you wish her to be addressed, or the next thing you know she is known as Gabby, Abby, or Brie.

A friend has a son named Andrew, who has not been, is not, nor ever will be referred to as Andy or Drew. His parents will make sure of it. If you feel strongly about this, you need to set the ground rules now, but do it nicely. Nothing is worse than an uptight parent copping an attitude because you called his child Ben instead of Benjamin.

Like, My Name Is Amy—with an "I"

Is your kid going to go through life constantly correcting people on how to spell his name? Some names are difficult enough without your taking creative license. Don't force your daughter to go through life saying, "I'm Tracy with two e's. Tracee."

Here's Pat

Is the name you choose a popular name for both boys and girls? If so, might this be a point of confusion later in life?

My wife and I violated this rule with both of our kids. My daughter Samantha is called Sam. My son's name, Skylar, is also a popular girl's name (spelled "Schuyler"). I have no idea how you get the pronunciation "Skylar" out of that spelling, but I'm a Hooked on Phonics kind of guy. We call him Sky. So when I tell people these are my kids, Sam and Sky, they are instantly confused about who is who.

I'll Pass on the Monogrammed Towels, Thanks

When selecting first and middle names, think about whether or not your child's initials spell something that would prevent him from ever wanting anything monogrammed later in life. I doubt that young Pamela Mary Smith (PMS) would want to have her initials on her gym bag or that Brandon Austin Davis (BAD) would want to have his initials embroidered on his shirt sleeves. However, you can be creative with initials if you choose. One friend, whose last name began with J, wanted to name his son Parker Brian so his initials would be PBJ, peanut butter and jelly.

In Honor of …

Different families, ethnic groups, and religions have traditions and customs for bestowing names as a way to honor someone. The most common way is to name your child after an actual family member. It can be either a first or middle name. Often, couples will take a wife's maiden name and make it the child's first or middle name or even modify it to make a new name, which is still in honor of the family or individual.

Certain groups feel different about naming a child after or in honor of someone while that person is still living. In the Jewish faith, it is customary not to give someone the name of a family member who is alive. It is considered a bad omen. If, however, there is a relative who has passed on that the family would like to honor, some people give the child a name beginning with the first letter of the honoree's name. For example, if I wanted to honor someone named Daniel, I could do so by naming a child David, Dylan, Dakota, or Doug. Pretty much anything except Damian, speaking of a bad *Omen.*

You can always honor yourself by making your little boy a "junior" or even a third, although most thirds with the exception of Thurston Howell III, eventually go by Trey. The notable exception is boxer George Foreman and his four sons, all named George Foreman.

Should We Tell People Our Choices?

It can be fun to talk about the names you've chosen. But it is a personal choice whether or not you want to tell people. Realize that by telling people your choices you are subjecting yourself to their opinions, whether you want them or not. Not everyone will be supportive. People will sometimes thoughtlessly trample on your choice.

My buddy Steve's wife was talking with a coworker who asked if they had selected a name for their son. Steve's wife responded, "Yes, we like Harrison." The coworker wrinkled her nose and said, "Yuck, not on my kid."

You may want to keep the name a surprise to prevent people from hassling you or as a way to honor or surprise family and friends on the big day. However, people will continue to hound you. Next time when someone asks, "Have you chosen a name?" one clever way to get around the question is to answer, "Sure, Gilligan if it's a boy and Mary Ann if it's a girl."

Your wife may elect not to tell anyone for fear of someone stealing the name. Yes, stealing the name. Let me tell you, brother, women take this seriously. Many of them have had names selected since they were little girls in pig tails and they are not about to risk an acquaintance, a cousin, or anyone else they know naming their child the same thing. It isn't like you can copyright these things or reserve them like an Internet domain address. It is more like an unspoken law of the jungle. Be prepared for tears if someone she knows suddenly takes her "dream" name.

When You Come Up with Nada

You can scour the books, hit the Web sites, and go through all of the characters in movies and literature, and still draw a blank. If this happens, you can always do what one couple did—draw letters out of a hat. Yes, they created their daughter's name the same way you would form a word in Scrabble. They drew seven letters out of a hat and assembled them to form the name Serette. Good thing they didn't get a *q* or *x*.

Actually, several books on the market are a great resource for possible names. A couple of the best are *Beyond Jennifer & Jason* and *The New American Dictionary of Baby Names*. You can also go to www.babycenter.com,

which has a unique baby-naming tool you can use.

Yeah, He Looks like a James

The last thing veteran daddies have to say about the name debate is that nothing is final until you put the name on the birth certificate. You and your wife reserve the right to change your mind at any point, including in the delivery room.

When my son was born, we had two names picked out that we really liked, but we couldn't decide. Rather than commit, we chose to wait and see what the baby looked like. If the baby was dark-haired and dark-skinned, we would name him one thing. If he had no hair or was fair, we would choose the other, which was more suited to a fair child. The name you have chosen may not fit the child once you see him or her. Be flexible and have backup choices.

DADDY SMARTS TOP TIPS on CHOOSING A NAME

- It is your duty as a rookie dad to make sure that the names selected meet stringent testing requirements, including the Nickname Test, the Playground Test, the Exotic Dancer Test, the Alternative Meanings Test, the Names That No One Can Possibly Live Up to Test, the Self-Fulfilling Prophecy Test, the Ex-Girlfriend's Name Test, the Ex-Boyfriend's Name Test, and the Bad Memory Test.

- Stay away from cutesy spellings and initials that may embarrass your child in the future.
- By telling people your choices, you are subjecting yourself to their opinions, whether you want them or not. People will sometimes react thoughtlessly to your choice.
- You may want to keep the name a surprise to prevent people from hassling you or as a way to honor or surprise family and friends on the big day.
- When someone asks, "Have you chosen a name?" one clever way to get around the question is to answer, "Sure, Gilligan if it's a boy and Mary Ann if it's a girl."
- If you can't agree on a name, scour the books, hit the web sites, think of characters in movies and literature, or draw letters out of a hat.

17

How Will We Raise Our Kids?

Your baby hasn't even been born yet and you and your wife are having a battle royal over things that won't affect him until he is a teenager. Your wife says, "I want him to go to State University." You respond with "That boy will be a Badger over my cold, dead body." Don't worry, you are perfectly normal.

You will have debates, discussions, and even fights about things ranging from whose turn it is to change a poopy diaper to where your child will go to college. And while you will fight passionately and fervently about these and other issues, there are only a few that really need to be decided before the birth of your child. Some of them might not even appear to affect a child until he or she is several years old. However, veteran daddies suggest that you and your spouse discuss and debate them ahead of time to avoid any problems once junior arrives. The following topics are only meant to give you some food for thought. Realize that there is no right

or wrong answer, only what is right for your family and your values, circumstances, beliefs, and budget.

Who Will Get Up in the Middle of the Night?

When your baby cries in the middle of the night, it is generally because he is wet, has gas, or is hungry. There can be other reasons, but these are the top three for newborns. If your wife breast-feeds, this is a fairly easy one. You are off the hook, my friend. Unless you have breasts, you are unequipped to handle this situation, so sweet dreams.

However, if you want to be Super Dad, you might offer to get the baby for your wife and bring him to bed so she can feed him more easily. For the first few weeks, don't be surprised if your baby is up every three hours or so.

If the child takes formula instead of breast-feeding, you and your wife may take turns getting up to warm bottles and feed the baby. The same goes if the child cries due to gas or because she needs her diaper changed. You may rotate throughout the night or decide to alternate nights.

Another thing you should consider is the workload or schedule each person has the next day. If your wife is not working or is still on maternity leave, she might not have anywhere to be early in the morning, but she may also have borne the brunt of the childcare duties all day long and might need some sleep to catch up. If you have a big day or meetings planned early the next morning, you should communicate this to your wife. Whether you choose to share duties or have one person be responsible for it all, remain flexible.

Will Your Wife Go Back to Work?

For many couples, this isn't even a choice. Your wife may want to stay home, but your family simply can't afford it. This can be rough on both your wife, who wants to be with the child, and on you, who may feel inadequate for not making enough money. You aren't alone. In over 60 percent of American families, both husband and wife work, often out of necessity. This is not an easy decision. For most people, it isn't as simple as saying "*Voila*, you are now a stay-at-home mom." There are financial and emotional factors to consider.

One of those considerations is insurance. If you filed the childbirth and pregnancy expenses through your wife's insurance, then she may have no choice but to return to work for a little while. While plans vary, most require that you return to work for at least thirty to sixty days. Otherwise, they can deny the claim and stick you with the bill. This is important to consider if she wants to quit working. She may have to return to work for a minimal period before resigning.

Does She Really Want to Stay at Home or Is It Your Ego?

Does she really want to stay home or do *you* want her to stay home? Where it was once large homes, cool cars, or trips, there is a growing trend in some large cities for the latest status symbol among young men to be able to say, "My wife stays at home." It implies "I'm doing so well she doesn't need to work." That may be great, but the fact of the matter is she may *want* to work. It's her choice.

She is a woman and all rights are reserved, including the right to change her mind on important matters. Don't be surprised if after the baby is born she changes how she feels about work. She may have planned to go back to work, but once the baby comes, she finds that she can't leave or she wants to go back only part-time. If she wants to stay at home but money is a concern, you might see if her employer offers flextime or if she would consider working part-time. However, the opposite may be true, and she may find that she wants to go back to work rather than stay home as a full-time mom.

You might think that staying at home would be a breeze. If you are fighting traffic to commute every day, playing politics at the office, or trying to meet an unbelievable deadline, then staying at home and being a full time mommy can sound like a great deal. But maternity leave serves as an excellent test run to see if your wife is cut out to stay at home.

My wife thought she wanted to stay at home. We were deliberating on whether or not we could afford it when she came to me about eight weeks into her maternity leave and said that she felt she couldn't do it. While she loved our daughter and loved spending time with her, she couldn't take the pace.

Will Our Kids Be in Day Care or Stay at Home?

If your wife stays at home, this is a subject you won't have to deal with until your child is about three or four and is old enough to attend preschool. However, if your wife is returning to work, you need to decide who will care for your child.

This is covered more extensively in "Child Care," but some things you and your wife should consider are whether or not you want your baby to be in a day care environment or if you would prefer for someone to come to your home to look after them. Do either of your employers offer on-site childcare or subsidy programs that offer discounted rates at local child care centers? Do you want to take your child to a person who cares for kids in her home? Does your church, temple, or mosque offer child care facilities? What can you afford that is available in your area?

Many tough choices lie ahead, and you need to decide this pretty quickly because you will need to reserve a space.

Public or Private School?

You have a while to go on this one too, but you and your wife can start to discuss it. Are you public school fans? Do you like the diversity and socialization that can come from a public school? Is the school system where you live highly regarded, or do they have problems? Did either of you go to private school, and if so, what was your experience? My wife went to private school and hated it, so she is opposed to our kids going to one. If you are thinking about private school, even preschool, you may need to get your name on a waiting list to reserve a spot. In New York and other cities, the exclusive preschools have a waiting list of several years. Parents try to get on the list the moment their child is born, or even sooner. Are you in favor of a religious or parochial school? Does your church, synagogue, temple, or mosque offer a private academy? And most important, can you afford it?

How Will We Discipline Our Kids?

Unless you are training a future marine, I don't think your baby is going to need a lot of discipline for a few months. When he does, starting around eighteen months, when he can start to grasp the concept, you and your wife need to decide how you are going to handle disciplining and correcting the child. There are many discipline methods and theories out there and I suggest that if you want to know more about the rationale behind them, read one of the several books on the subject.

The three most common methods of discipline are time-out (standing in the corner or leaving the room), losing privileges (taking something of value away), and corporal punishment (otherwise known as "spanking"). I'm not here to tell you what to do or recommend one way over another. Personally, I'm *not* a spanker, although a three-year-old can make you think twice. You might be thinking, "My mom spanked *my* little behind and I turned out all right." Great. But times and opinions have changed regarding spanking.

If you and your wife do not see eye-to-eye on discipline, there can be problems when the child is old enough to need it. You and your wife should sit down and discuss your options to find common ground. You both need to think about your temperament, the rationale behind your type of discipline, and what messages you're sending to the child.

Choosing a Religion

If you and your wife are of the same faith and denomination, then it's a snap. However, if you are of different denominations or especially of different faiths, this can be a real headache, not only for you but also for both sets of grandparents. Actually, how the child will be raised, christened, baptized, or named is often a much bigger deal to grandparents than parents. This is a highly personal choice fraught with tension.

In interfaith marriages, experts and clergy are in favor of giving the child one religious identity. Later in life, that child may end up choosing one religion over the other, but it can be confusing for a small child not to have one identity. A five-, eight- or even ten-year-old can't understand "I'm Jewish *and* I'm Christian" or "I'm Catholic *and* Baptist."

In some faiths, including Judaism, the child's religion is determined by the mother. If the mother is Jewish, the baby is Jewish. Also, some clergy make interfaith couples agree to raise a child a certain way as a condition of marrying them.

These are things to consider, but ultimately you and your wife will have to do what is right for your family. If your decision risks upsetting a relative or family member, you should weigh it carefully. Both of you should talk with the family member about your choice, explain your position, and hope for his support.

Choosing Godparents

If your faith or family tradition supports godparents, you and your wife have a big choice to make. The idea of godparents means different things to different families. It is often an honor bestowed on a close family friend. Some families view the godparent as the person responsible for the child's religious education. Others see godparents as surrogate parents who will care for the child if you die.

And finally, some people think of godparents simply as an unrelated aunt or uncle, kind of like having a close family friend called Uncle Bob.

The role godparents play in your child's life is up to you and your wife. When choosing a godparent for your child, consider the long-term relationship. Is this a person you will still be close to in twenty years, or will it be like your wedding pictures—"I don't talk to half these people anymore"?

It might not make sense to give the godparent designation to an immediate family member. After all, the grandparents, aunts, and uncles already *have* important roles, naturally.

Who Will Take Care of Our Child If We Die?

This is a tough subject, especially since everything regarding birth has to do with life and happy thoughts. But this is one of the responsibilities of being a parent. Most couples select one of their own sets of parents or a sibling. Others elect godparents or close friends to care for the child.

When selecting someone, consider that person's emotional and financial stability. Are their values the same as yours? Do they value education as you do? Is that person overburdened with his or her own health problems? Would your child be an overwhelming burden for someone barely making ends meet or in an unstable marriage? Will that person love and raise your child as you would? Not easy stuff to think about.

After you and your wife identify

someone whom you would feel comfortable with, you should talk with her and tell her of your choice. Ask if she would be willing to accept such a responsibility.

As soon as the child is born, you need to prepare a will. They can be prepared very simply and cheaply through an attorney, or you can even get forms from the Web. But this is something that you shouldn't put off.

Do We Need to Change Our Lifestyle?

Having a child makes you readjust your priorities. You may need to change some things. You can still have fun, but there is another human who not only depends on you for survival, but who needs you to provide a comfortable, positive environment.

If your wife stays home or cuts back on her hours, some adjustments will have to be made. You may also have to take a look at your current travel schedule, social activities, and even hobbies. You must evaluate the type of people and influences you are surrounded by. You or your spouse may choose to quit smoking, drinking, or skydiving. Who knows? Do what is right for you and your family, but at least take time to evaluate your lifestyle, and ask yourself if you and your spouse are acting in your family's best interest.

Talk about these things early. When the baby arrives, things move so quickly that you won't have time or energy to deal with them without putting undue pressure on your self. The key is to remain flexible and open to change along the way.

DADDY SMARTS TOP TIPS on
RAISING YOUR KIDS

- Realize that there is no right or wrong answer, only what is right for your family and your values, circumstances, beliefs, and budget.
- To avoid any confusion, discuss the following questions before the birth of your child.
  Who will get up in the middle of the night?
  Will your wife go back to work?
  Will our kids be in day care or stay at home?
  How will we discipline our kids?
  Who will take care of our child if we die?
  Do we need to change our lifestyle?
- If your choice of faith for the child risks upsetting a relative or family member, you should weigh it carefully. Both of you should talk with the family member about your choice, explain your position, and hope for his support.

18

Child Care

What is your most precious possession? How do you take care of it? Now multiply that care and attention by ten—you still can't even begin to understand how important day care is. Finding someone who will take proper care of your bear cub, without sending you to the poorhouse, is the most nerve-racking experience parents go through. And it's ongoing. Every couple I know has at least one or two child care issues come up every year. Whether it is poor care, a change in quality or price, a child who is a bad influence, your kid *being* the bad influence, or the departure of a favorite teacher or care giver, the problems never seem to stop. They go on and on.

Frankly, child care, whether day care or bringing someone in your home, will scare the hell out of you. This is not like leaving your new car with a careless valet. Your child is the most precious, irreplaceable thing in the world.

I don't envy caregivers. I admire and appreciate the good ones, as

should you. Caring for a child is the toughest job in the world, yet many of these people make only six or eight dollars an hour. They are often overworked, underappreciated, and (unfortunately) untrained.

There are many options, and as with many of the decisions you and your wife have to make, there is not one right or wrong choice. Each type of care depends on your preference and your budget. Below are basics on the types of care available, and some things you should consider when choosing a provider.

Essentially, you have three options. First, there is day care in a formal school or center setting. This can be through a local school or center or a national chain such as KinderCare. Some churches, temples, and religious organizations also provide care at their facilities. Then there is child care provided by an individual in her own home: there are people who keep one or several kids in their home during the day. And finally, there is child care in your own home. This can be through a full- or part-time nanny.

Each has its pros, cons, and points to consider.

Day Care Centers and Home Providers

When you are evaluating a day care center or home provider, you should first consider location, security, cleanliness, cost, and teacher-to-child ratio. Both you and your wife should make it a point to visit the provider during a regular day when children are there.

Visit the caregiver or the facility unannounced. This is key. Don't set an appointment. You want to see how things really are at any given moment. Read: total chaos.

A center may have a beautiful building and a cute logo or name, but what really matters is beneath the surface. When you walk around, are kids crying uncontrollably and being neglected? Are kids hitting one another, with no one correcting them? Can you easily walk around or gain entrance before someone stops you and asks what you are doing there? Does the place smell like urine or unchanged diapers? Are wires exposed? Is paint peeling or chipping? Are there bugs? Does the furniture or play equipment appear clean, reasonably new, and safe? Are older kids (ages four, five, and six) in contact with smaller kids and babies? This is important to know when your two-year-old comes home swearing like a sailor because she learned it from "the big kids."

Is there a lot of turnover among staff? How long has the staff been there? Watch the teachers with the children. Are they playing with the babies or are they sitting around talking with each other? Babies need attention and stimulus. Do the teachers sing or talk to the babies? Is the music being played in the nursery appropriate, such as lullabies, classical, or children's music or is Garth Brooks turned up full blast like it's Saturday night at Billy Bob's honky tonk? This actually was the case at one center we saw.

How many babies do they have in the room? The law varies from state to state, but there are regulations that limit how many children one teacher may care for. In Texas, one teacher is allowed to care for up to six babies under one year old. I think that is ridiculously high, but that is the law. Some centers have smaller ratios such as four-to-one or five-to-one.

Does that give you enough to think about? Wait, there's more. If you call now, you'll also get … to worry about background checks. Make sure that the provider performs criminal background checks on their employees. You should also ask if they perform those checks nationwide or just in your state. Some only run checks in-state, yet a person may have committed a crime in another part of the country.

Questions to Ask

Is your provider insured and bonded? Also look for security measures. Do parents need a door code to enter the building? Are there passwords needed for a person other than Mom or Dad to pick up a child? Are there video cameras in the classrooms? Ask if they actually record, or if they are for monitoring only. It doesn't do a damn bit of good to have a camera if there is no film to catch someone doing something—or not doing something, like failing to take care of your kid. Make sure that the center allows you to drop in anytime. If they do not let you come in unannounced, then find another provider. You should be able to see your child anytime without advance warning. If I sound a little passionate or uptight about this, it's because I am. And you will be too. Just wait.

A Word about In-Home Providers

Veteran daddies advise against leaving your child with a caregiver who also cares for her own kids. In many cases, there are no problems, but think about it. Whose kid will she be most interested in? Also, what if her kid is sick? In most day care centers, if a kid is sick, that child must stay home to prevent him from getting everyone else sick. Where does the caregiver's sick child go? Some in-home providers with a sick child call the parents to tell them not to bring their kids. That is the responsible thing to do, so every child isn't sick, but it sure sucks having to take a vacation day because someone else's child is sick and you are stuck without child care.

National Chains versus Local Day Care

You may choose between a nationally or locally owned day care center. There are several fine national day care chains such as KinderCare. They are no better or worse than a locally owned or parochial day care. However, you should still check out each individual location. Many are franchised, so quality can vary from location to location.

Religious Day Care

Many churches, temples, and other religious organizations offer short-term day care, often called Mommy and Me or Mommy's Day Out. This is often provided for a half day or for several hours and is offered only a few days a week. It is an opportunity for parents to drop their kid off and have some time to spend alone or to run some errands, but it is not intended to be a regular day care. Some religious centers do offer full-time day care.

Employer-Provided Opportunities

If your employer offers on-site day care at work, this may be the best option for you and your wife. Companies who offer this benefit to employees usually outsource the care to a private company. Employees are charged fees that are substantially less than those for outside or private child care. The benefits are that you or your wife can visit the child throughout the day, which can be especially helpful if your wife is breast-feeding. The challenge is being able to reserve a spot. These are so popular that there may not be room for your child.

Some employers have made arrangements with local day care providers for their employees to receive a discounted rate. Ask your company's human resources or benefits department if they have such arrangements or if you can get them to negotiate a rate for employees.

Visit, Visit, Visit

Whether you are considering a day care center or an in-home provider, make sure that both you and your wife visit the caregiver several times. You can give a lot of weight to reputation and word of mouth, but when it comes down to it, you must trust your gut.

Our first visit to a day care center was almost enough to make me stay at home and become Mr. Mom. My wife and I visited a local center with one of my wife's coworkers, Cheryl, and her husband, Kevin. They were expecting their first child a few weeks after us and so we all decided to tour a child care center near my wife's office.

We approached a green, run-down building that used to be a house and were able to walk directly in the front door, which was unlocked. There was no gate, receptionist, or waiting area, just kids playing everywhere. The place smelled musty and old.

There was not an adult in sight, but I saw a roomful of two- or three-year-olds off to the side. There was a temporary gate blocking the door of the room. One little boy was attempting to climb the gate, which gave way. He came tumbling down with the gate on top of him.

As I walked over to help the boy, a woman came from inside the room and jerked the little boy into the air by one arm. She noticed me and put on a fake smile, "Can I help you?" My wife said that we wanted to talk to the director about enrolling our newborns. "She's on the phone. Just a minute and I'll get her."

About five minutes later, a woman in her fifties, wearing the shortest shorts I've ever seen on a woman that age, came out and said, "I'm sorry to keep you all waiting. I was on the phone with Child Protective Services. You know how they can be." I shot my wife and the other couple a look of surprise and thought, "No lady. I don't know how they are and I hope never to find out."

In Texas, Child Protective Services is the agency that monitors child abuse, pulls kids out of abusive and neglected homes, and looks out for children's welfare. It wasn't a vote of confidence to hear that this woman apparently dealt with them on a semi-regular basis and didn't appear to be thrilled about it. I looked at Kevin, who had the same disgusted look I did. We turned around, walked out, and waited for our wives in the car.

After much searching, we ultimately found a day care we were happy with. It was close to my wife's work, the equipment was new, they had great security, and the staff appeared to be caring. The cribs in the baby room were beautiful classic-style wooden cribs that were either new or had been refurbished to pristine condition.

Life at this day care facility was great for about six months. Then my wife called one day after picking up Samantha. She was very upset and could barely get the words out: "They are keeping our daughter in a cage." I said to calm down, it couldn't be that bad. I went to the day care the next day and discovered that my wife was right. The owner had moved the beautiful cribs to another room for older kids to use, and in their place she had put two sets of stackable cribs.

These are space-saving devices designed to be stacked one on top of the other. They look like a wooden box except that two of the sides are made of wooden slats. The remainder of the crib is solid. Since you can't put the child into the crib from the top, your only option is to lift one of the slatted sides to put the child in. When closed, it looks like a kennel cage. We didn't like them at all.

I certainly didn't want my daughter completely enclosed in something and I also didn't want her only view to be bars or the top of the next kid's crib. I could see Sam in twenty years at the therapist: "I was raised like a caged animal." We were also concerned that the cribs could fall. It was awful.

We weren't the only ones to complain either. Every parent with a baby in that room had called the center director, who responded by saying, "There is nothing wrong with those cribs. We were able to get those cribs on sale. It is a business decision and I'm sticking with it." As parents we made a business decision too, and every parent pulled their kid out of the center within a week.

Nannies and Home Providers

If you are thinking about hiring a nanny to care for your child in your own home, you need to first decide if you want a full-time, live-in nanny or one who only cares for your child during the day.

There are obvious benefits to having a nanny over placing your child in a day care facility. First, your child will receive more individual attention than he would in a class with a five-to-one or six-to-one teacher-to-child ratio. He also will not be exposed to as many of the germs and viruses commonly found in day care. Kids in day care seem to get sick much more frequently than those who are not. Another benefit is that your child is cared for in your own home, making it easier on him and you. Of course, all of this care comes at a price, one that is often much more than that of day care.

Nanny fees vary depending on your location and on the skills and qualifications you require. It is almost comical to hear couples discuss the market value for nannies' particular skills. If you want one who speaks English, it costs more. If you want one who knows how to drive and has a license, you will pay even more. And if you want one who speaks English, can drive, and has her own car, then you had better think about a second mortgage.

Prices can range anywhere from $300 to $800 per week. Some couples choose to pay for health insurance for their nanny. Since you are employing a nanny, you are expected to pay employer's taxes and social security, which add to the overall cost. You can of course choose not to pay those taxes, but you are running a costly risk by doing so, not to mention jeopardizing any hopes of ever becoming a Supreme Court Justice.

Similar to a nanny is an au pair. This is often a young girl in her late teens or twenties, who comes to the United States from another country to live with a family and care for their children. The costs are similar to a regular nanny. There are services who set up such arrangements. You can learn about many though the Web. Some people choose to use an au pair and have a great experience. However, remember that these are often college-age girls who may be away from home in the United States for the first time. Critics caution that some au pairs may not be very experienced or may become undependable once they arrive in the United States and discover the night life.

Some questions that you should ask when evaluating a potential nanny include: Does she have reliable transportation? Does she drive? Does she speak English? Does she smoke? Will she take care of minor household chores, or is she a nanny only? Will you allow your nanny to have guests? Does she have experience? What is her background? Does she have any references?

People find nannies either through word of mouth or through agencies that place nannies with families. You can find great information about locating a nanny as well as information about taxes, legal requirements, and contracts at www.babycenter.com. This site also has a great day care locator, which will help you find a provider in your area.

Jacob, a dad in St. Louis, tells about a caregiver he and his wife brought into their home. "A friend recommended her to us. She was a cousin of their nanny. She had just arrived from Russia, and I was told that she spoke little English. We were surprised at how little. When she arrived, she simply smiled a lot and said her name was Olga. She apparently was a smoker, because she smelled like a Russian tobacco factory. She did a great job, but when I went to pick up my daughter several hours after Olga left, my daughter smelled like the Marlboro man."

Should We Set Up a Camera?

Security is a huge concern any time you bring someone into your home. There are now companies that rent hidden cameras and recording equipment. They will come in and install it for you. Prices vary but you are looking at between $100 to $200 for a couple of days to a week. There are no laws prohibiting this, but if you have a live-in nanny, you must respect her room and privacy.

You may want to use taping for your own for peace of mind, especially if you notice anything unusual with your child, such as bumps, bruises, marks, or significant changes in behavior. You may feel like a snoop, but this is your child we're talking about. If the worst thing that happens is that you feel like a heel for checking up on your nanny, then consider yourself lucky. The news is full of stories where a child care provider was either harmful or negligent. Most caregivers are fantastic and my family is currently blessed with some great ones. But you and your wife will have to decide.

Take a Test Drive

Before you make a long-term commitment to a nanny or caregiver, take her for a test drive to see how she performs. While your wife is still on maternity leave and at home, ask the nanny candidate if she could baby-sit for you once to see how it goes. You will pay her, of course. You or your wife can even be at home taking a nap or doing something around the house while the nanny cares for the baby. This will give you a chance to see how the caregiver responds to the baby and if she is attentive.

Baby-Sitters

Even though this chapter has dealt with day care, there is still another kind of care you need to think about for your child: baby-sitters. When you find a good baby-sitter, treat her like gold.

I'll let you in on a couple of secrets about baby-sitters. The best place to find one is at your child's day care center. Start by asking his day care teacher if she baby-sits on the side. If not, ask if there are other teachers in the center who like to baby-sit. The teachers are likely to know your child, and he is probably comfortable around them. You will also know how to find them easily, and know that criminal and background checks have been done by the day care center.

One person you will *not* want to consider as a baby-sitter, at least in the beginning, is a neighborhood teenage girl. You may know a friend's daughter or other young teenager who would be a great sitter. That's okay. Just don't use her until your baby is older. Infants require special care. It can be overwhelming even for the most mature parent, let alone a teenager, when a baby is inconsolable. Also, if there is a problem, you want her to be able to drive and handle herself in an emergency.

DADDY SMARTS TOP TIPS **on CHILD CARE**

- When evaluating a day care center or home provider, consider location, security, cleanliness, costs, and teacher-to-child ratio.
- A center may have a beautiful building and a cute logo or name, but what really matters is beneath the surface.
- Veteran daddies advise against leaving your child with a caregiver who also cares for her own kids.
- Many national chains are franchised, so quality can vary from location to location.
- Visit the provider during a regular day when children are there. You can give a lot of weight to reputation and word of mouth, but when it comes down to it, trust your gut.
- Before you make a long-term commitment to a nanny or caregiver, have her baby-sit to see how she performs.

Labor Day

If you think that Labor Day means cooking on the grill, water-skiing, a three-day weekend, and the end of summer, forget it.

This is the Labor Day that you will never forget. This section features everything from going to the hospital to taking your newest family member home.

Now turn the page, and don't forget to "breathe, baby, breathe!"

19

Be Prepared: Getting Ready for Labor Day

The Boy Scout motto is "Be Prepared." Unfortunately, there isn't a merit badge for being a daddy and going through childbirth ... unless you were a really *naughty* Boy Scout.

Nine months of suspense and buildup can sure creep up on you. One day you are looking at a red positive sign in a plastic square, with someone telling you that you are going to be a daddy, and the next thing you know you are getting a 911 page from your wife to meet her at the hospital: she's in labor. All of your waiting, anxiety, and anticipation prepare you for this moment. This is not a test. Within twenty-four to thirty-six hours or less, you, my friend, can add the title Daddy to your resume.

Regardless of how prepared you think you are, you are going to be blindsided when you get the actual call from your wife or the nudge in the middle of the night to grab the keys and warm the car up. To make sure that you aren't caught off guard, you should consider the following tips.

Pack a Daddy Bag

Your wife has probably had her bag packed long ago. It will contain nightgowns, makeup, chapstick, nursing bras, and other items that she will need to make her stay more comfortable. But you should pack a bag too. Even if you don't spend the night at the hospital after your child is born, you are going to be there a long time. Remember, labor and delivery can take up to twenty-four hours or more.

Bring a fresh change of clothes and make sure that they are comfortable. Throw in some jeans, tennis shoes, and maybe a sweatshirt. When I got the page from my wife to meet her at the hospital, I rushed to the delivery room still dressed in a suit. Our child wasn't born until almost ten hours later. Fortunately, a friend brought me some casual clothes—but forgot to bring shoes. For almost twenty-four hours, I was in jeans and incredibly uncomfortable wing-tipped dress shoes.

You are going to be there a long

time. If your wife has the baby in the middle of the night, chances are that your dining options are bad coffee, sodas, and snack food from a vending machine. Many hospital cafeterias or snack bars aren't open twenty-four hours a day.

Be sure to stick in some chips, candy, sodas, water, gum, Power Bars—whatever you want to give you energy and get you through. Try not to take foods that smell or have a pungent odor. While delicious, I'm sure your wife won't appreciate the beef jerky you've been eating just before you help her with her breathing exercises.

If you or a guest bring in fast food, make sure to eat it outside of your wife's room. The smells can still make her sick. In addition, you're torturing her because she can't eat anything. Women aren't allowed to eat solid food or drink during labor. Many hospitals only let women eat ice chips or Popsicles, which are often available in the nurse's coffee or break area.

Bring some of you and your wife's favorite CDs. Most labor and delivery rooms have CD players and stereos. Make sure to bring a mix of musical styles. It helps to bring something instrumental and soothing. Classical or new age music works really well while your wife is pushing or breathing through difficult contractions. Bring something that reminds her of when you got married or other sentimental occasions.

Many labor and delivery rooms also have VCR units. Some people really enjoy popping in a video to take their attention off of the waiting, or in some cases the pain. It is up to you. We made a point of buying the video of *Babe* and schlepping it to the hospital, only never to turn the TV on.

Take a toothbrush, hairbrush, deodorant, and even a razor. You don't want to look like a terrorist in your first picture with your baby. Besides, you will feel better after the long hours of waiting if you can freshen up a bit.

Stock the Kitchen

After the baby arrives, your wife will not feel like cooking at all, assuming she cooked before the baby was born. Even if you are a good cook and handle all of the culinary activities, you will not have the time or motivation to cook or even go to the grocery store.

Veteran daddies suggest that you go to the grocery store around the due date and load up on staples. Try to keep a surplus of food and supplies around the house so you won't have to keep running out to the store, at least for the first couple of weeks.

A really smart idea is to prepare several dishes and freeze them a few weeks before the baby arrives. Lasagna, stew, spaghetti sauce, or casseroles work well. After you make the dish, pack it in single serving sizes for your wife and you. This way you won't have to heat up a giant lasagna that will go bad in a few days.

House Sitters

Do you have a neighbor you can call or someone who can look after your house, get your paper, bring in the mail, turn on the lights, and feed your dog while you're at the hospital? Let a couple of people in your neighborhood know when the due date is near. Ask if they can help you out. Give them a key so that when the big day arrives, there won't be any confusion and you can focus on what's important, your wife and child.

Car Seat and Baby Items

You should have made your arrangements for the nursery and baby furniture before now. If you have, fantastic. If you have purchased everything and it only needs to be delivered, you should call the store close to the due date or when your wife goes into labor to make sure that they can deliver it before you arrive home.

You should also confirm that they will assemble anything that needs to be put together. Getting home to find your baby's crib is still in a box sucks, to say the least. It is worth the extra cost to have someone move and assemble any furniture, because in about two days, when you bring junior home, you are going to be about as useful as a ball of lint and in no mood to put together baby furniture.

You should also have already purchased a car seat. If you remember anything, remember this: You can't take the baby home without a car seat. It might even be smart for you to put it in the car you plan to bring everyone home from the hospital in. The moment your wife and child are being wheeled out of the hospital is the wrong time to learn how to put the seat in. Also, make sure the straps are adjusted for the smallest setting, so your baby will fit securely and safely.

Pager and Cell Phones

How you and your wife communicate during this period is critical. This is especially true if your job requires travel. If you have a cellular or digital phone, you should keep it with you at all times. If you do not have a cell phone, you should consider getting one. Many companies offer inexpensive "safety plans" for people who need infrequent or emergency-only use. A pager is a great inexpensive option.

If you travel, make sure that your phone or pager will work in the region you are roaming or traveling in. Having a cell phone is useless if your service only works while you are in town.

You should leave the numbers where you can be reached prominently displayed at home and at your office. Your wife should also carry a card with these numbers, so she can have someone contact you if she is incapacitated.

Some couples who use pagers have numerical codes that communicate certain things, such as "Call me back," "I'm okay," or "911"—which means, "Meet me at the hospital. This is it."

As the due date nears, you should

also keep your phone and pager on at all times. And check your voice mail religiously. If your phone rings in a meeting, apologize and explain that your wife is pregnant and this could be it. People will understand.

Routes

You should map out several routes for getting to the hospital. If you live in a large city, you should take traffic into consideration. Plan one route that can be used in case you have to go to the hospital during rush hour and another route that can be taken at night or during a nonpeak period.

Call Lists

You and your wife should have already thought about who you want to come to the hospital and be there for the birth. You should prepare a list of people to call so that the moment you go to the hospital you, or someone else, can let everyone know.

Are your parents and in-laws in town or are they going to fly in? What about siblings and close friends? Have you made arrangements for someone to keep your other children or pick them up from day care? Are there people who won't come to the hospital but that you want to let know that your wife is in labor? This can include close friends, coworkers, or nonimmediate family. Of course, you don't *have* to let all of these people know that your wife is in labor. If you want, you can wait to tell them after the baby is born.

Labor Day Checklist

- Do you have your wife? (Hey, just checking.)
- Camera! Camera! Camera!
- Film, film, film. (It would be a bonehead move to forget this.)
- Video camera, film, battery, and a tripod if the doctor allows videotaping.
- Do you have your call list?
- Does your wife have her bag?
- Do you have your bag?
- Do you have comfortable clothes?
- Do you have a cell phone or calling card?
- Do you have snacks?
- Do you have all of your hospital forms and insurance info?
- Have you settled on a name?
- Have you purchased a car seat for the ride home?

Should Your Wife Drive Herself?

Yeah, and you should enjoy the ride and listen to sports radio. Of course your first choice is for *you* to be able to drive your wife to the hospital, but that is not always possible. Depending upon the frequency and severity of your wife's contractions, she may be perfectly fine driving herself. However, contractions can change in severity very quickly. The worst thing that can happen is for your wife to be driving on a freeway when she has a contraction that doubles her over in pain. Have a friend, coworker, or neighbor who is on call drive your wife to the hospital if you aren't around.

Hurry Up and Wait

The last few days of the pregnancy, your wife is likely to be incredibly uncomfortable. She is also probably sick and tired of people asking questions like, "When are you due?" and "You haven't had that baby yet?" She may also be anxious about the baby's health. The bottom line is that she is edgy. Let's just say that she is not the only one who wants to hurry up and have this baby. Toward the end, she may be moodier and more emotional than ever. She will feel the baby's impending arrival and she will be second-guessing herself and kicking herself for not getting more done or not taking better care of herself. And as luck would have it, she may kick you too. Hang in there.

If you relied on movies and TV as your only source of childbirth knowledge, you would think that the moment a woman had her first contraction it is a mad drag race across town to get to the hospital before the baby's head pops out. Contrary to TV births, the real thing does not take ten minutes and most children are not crowning or being born within seconds of the woman reaching the operating room.

We all have all heard the stories of the frantic husband, running through red lights and being a menace to society to get his wife to the hospital before she explodes. The truth is that you are more likely to freak out than your wife is. Take your time and be safe. This does not mean that you should stop off at McDonald's or get the mail. If your wife's contractions are consistently less than five minutes apart, you should get a move on.

All women are different, but it can take a long time for a woman's contractions to reach a certain frequency. However, while she can remain dilated at a certain point for a long time, things can also change quickly and dramatically. Some women rapidly go from being dilated at four centimeters to eight or nine. It doesn't always happen like that, but once a woman is dilated past seven or eight, it won't be long before she starts pushing the baby out.

The Night Before

If your wife's labor is scheduled to be induced, you won't have that "Oh, my gosh, what do I do?" experience, but you do get the distinct pleasure the night before of being with your wife who is on pins and needles. Our second child was two weeks late, so we scheduled an induction. That evening Meredith began "nesting." She thought *now* would be a good time to clean the closet, and it sent her into orbit that certain things weren't done yet. She was on a rampage and there was nothing I could do to calm her down.

What finally did it was that I made posters for her, using pictures of our daughter and our soon-to-be-born son's sonogram pictures. I used my computer and made signs with the pictures attached. One was a picture of my daughter that said, "Bring me back something special from the hospital." I hung it on the back door for her to see as she was leaving the house the next morning. Another sign displayed the sonogram picture of our son with the words, "Hi, Mommy, come and get me." I placed it on the mirror by her sink. She loved them and finally loosened up. We still have those pictures up to this day.

When You Get the Call

You have thought long and hard about this moment. You have planned for it and have even acted out what you will say, do, and feel when it arrives. But now that it is here, you don't know how to react. Relax, you are perfectly normal. When your wife calls, pages, or nudges you to let you know that it's time, you will be caught completely off guard and will react differently than you anticipated.

Your wife may be surprisingly calm or screaming at the top of her lungs. She may simply say, "This is it," or "Meet me at the hospital. I love you. Bye." But that message will change your life.

For some reason, however, these calls come at the most inopportune moments. I made it a point to stay in town for the weeks leading up to the birth of our first child. I was scheduled to speak at a luncheon close to the due date. We agreed that since it was in town, this was not a problem. The scheduled luncheon speakers were myself and the mayor, but earlier that morning the mayor was forced to cancel. I was sitting at the luncheon, about twenty minutes

before I was to speak to a roomful of about two hundred people already upset that the mayor had cancelled, when I got the 911 page from my wife.

We had agreed that this page would be a "drop everything and go to the hospital" page. I had just purchased the pager, and this was the first time other than a test that it had beeped. The buzz about sent me through the roof I was so jittery. I looked at the pager and leaned over to my hosts, who knew my situation, and apologized. The one in a million shot of my wife going into labor while I was speaking had just happened. The group was very understanding and they asked me back the following year, assuming my wife was not pregnant.

False Alarms

Don't be surprised if once or even several times near the due date, you have a false start. Your wife looks at you and swears that this is it. She is having frequent strong contractions, so you go to the hospital thinking that she is in labor. After all, she is showing all the signs.

Once you arrive at the hospital, the nurse will likely check your wife out internally to see how dilated her cervix is, and she will strap a fetal monitor on your wife to see how the baby is doing. Once the nurse checks your wife, she is likely to say that they want to wait an hour or so to see if anything happens. If things progress and she becomes more dilated, congratulations, she is in labor.

If not, then it was likely a condition called Braxton Hicks, or false labor. It is fairly common and most women can tell the difference between Braxton Hicks contractions and the real thing. But it is not unusual for a woman to mistake it for actual labor. Time to get dressed and go home. This was not it.

It is a huge buildup and a crushing letdown, but it happens to many people. Your wife is going to feel like an idiot. Pure and simple. But in fact nothing could be further from the truth. She did the right thing in going to the hospital. If you have insurance, it cost you nothing. It is always better to be safe than sorry. Nonetheless, she will feel stupid and embarrassed. It is your job to reassure her that she did the right thing by going to the hospital.

You may be a little upset because you were mentally set that this would be the day. Don't worry about it. Think of it as a false start. Now you at least know a little better how you will react.

DADDY SMARTS TOP TIPS **on GETTING READY FOR LABOR DAY**

- Pack a daddy bag. Bring a fresh change of clothes and make sure that they are comfortable. Throw in some jeans, tennis shoes, and maybe a sweatshirt and snacks.
- Bring some of you and your wife's favorite CDs. Most labor and delivery rooms have CD players and stereos.
- Take a toothbrush, hairbrush, deodorant, and even a razor. You don't want to look like a terrorist in your first picture with your baby.
- Try to keep a surplus of food and supplies around the house so you won't have to keep running out to the store, at least for the first couple of weeks.
- Can someone look after your house, get your paper, bring in the mail, turn on the lights, and feed your dog while you're at the hospital? Let a couple of people in your neighborhood know when the due date is near.
- Make sure that any furniture is delivered before you arrive home.
- Put the car seat in the car you plan to bring everyone home from the hospital in.
- Leave the numbers where you can be reached prominently displayed at home and at your office.
- Keep your phone and pager on at all times. And check your voice mail religiously.
- Plan one route that can be used in case you have to go to the hospital during rush hour and another route that can be taken at night or during a nonpeak period.
- Don't be surprised if once or even several times near the due date, you have a false start.

20

Hospital Smarts, Part 1

Two couples check into the hospital at the same time. Both give birth to healthy children without any complications, yet one couple has a great experience at the hospital and the other couple swears that they will never come back. What went wrong?

In many ways, delivering a child at a hospital is not all that different from going to a restaurant, in that the service you receive can make or break your experience. Veteran daddies agree that there are a few simple things you can do to ensure that your wife receives good service and that your experience is memorable for all the right reasons.

You Don't Ask, You Don't Get

"He who asks ... gets." When you and your wife arrive at the hospital and discover that a certain room that you would like is open, then ask for it. Otherwise, you are at the mercy of where the nurses assign you. And be polite. It is like your mother used to say: "Ask, don't tell." Saying, "Could we please have this room?" works

much better than "We want that room."

When you arrive and get your wife settled into her room, be sure to check out where everything is. Take a quick reconnaissance tour to discover where the nursery is, locate the cafeteria, and discover where the nurses' break room is so you can get Popsicles or ice chips for your wife. You should also take notice of the waiting areas, phones, and parking so you can tell your family and friends where to go when they arrive. If they offer parking tokens to fathers, make sure to get a handful of them so you don't have to keep going back for more. You can also give a few to your family.

One other area you should be aware of when you arrive is the big status board located by the nurses' station. It is an enormous white marker board that gives the status of every mother and baby currently checked in. It lists the patient's name, their doctor, how dilated the mother is, and other information that tells how close she is to giving birth.

How to Make Sure Your Wife Gets Great Service

The men and women on the staff deal with dozens of crazy, stressed out, and clueless people every day, all of whom think that the sun rises and sets according to their schedule. Don't worry—this isn't a bad thing. The day their child is born entitles everyone to be a little selfish. However, the staff see it several times a day, so after a while the shine and newness wear off, particularly when they get screamed at on a semiregular basis by clueless dads such as you.

The key to getting great service at the hospital is simple but effective: be nice. As the cliché says, "You catch more flies with honey than vinegar." If you are sweet, patient, and even appear a little naive (if you are a rookie dad), of course the nursing staff is much more likely to help you and to remember your wife positively.

How to Make Sure Your Wife Is Ignored

On the other hand, if you are a demanding, yelling, screaming, tyrannical jerk who berates the staff because "We called five minutes ago and nobody has come to see my wife, who is in pain, dammit!" then you and your wife certainly *will* be remembered. You will be remembered as that obnoxious couple who can wait until the nurses are damn good and ready. Equally ineffective is name dropping and threatening: "We know Joe Blow, who sits on the board of this hospital." Big deal. It doesn't matter who you know or what you

threaten. At that moment, when your wife and baby's care is in these people's hands, then the nursing staff are the most powerful people you need to know.

If you do make an ass out of yourself, swallow your pride, say you're sorry, and make amends. Immediately go apologize to the staff for your behavior and blame it on stress and being an idiot.

Greasing the Wheel

Are you a schmoozer? Have you ever taken a client to lunch or given out tickets to a ball game or other perk? What did you hope to accomplish by doing this? You wanted to win their favor. The same concept works for the nurses and staff caring for your wife.

While they are not allowed to take money or gifts, they are allowed to eat. I'm here to tell you that the best $20 investment you will ever make is the pizzas, bagels, Chinese food, or other take-out you will buy for the nursing staff on duty. Ask the main nurse caring for your wife if she and the rest of the staff would like anything in particular, as you are going to have something delivered. You can also have a friend or family member pick up something on their way to the hospital. The nurses will really appreciate it and will remember you and your wife.

Get Personal

You and your wife are about to share one of the most personal experiences in a lifetime with someone you have just met: your wife's main nurse. Ask her name and go out of your way to introduce yourself and tell her a little bit about you and your wife. Make it a point to learn a little bit about her (or him). She is going to help you become a family in a very short time and you will remember her for a long time to come. Your wife will be the lead person in developing this relationship, but you can do a lot to help make an advocate out of the nurse.

If you get a great nurse, you should hope that she has just started her shift. Your wife could be there a long time and might deliver long after your new best friend has gone home. Ask her when her shift is over so you know. Once they change shifts, you will get a different nurse and you will have to go through all of this rapport-building again.

When Things Go Sour

Although this is the biggest day in your life up to this point, it is a routine workday to the staff and the doctors, who deliver thousands of babies each year. Beyond any of the complications that can occur involving your wife's or the baby's health, everyday things can and occasionally do occur to rain on your parade. Here are a few of those things and how you can deal with them if they occur.

All the Great Rooms Are Full

Remember the hospital tour a couple of months ago? You and your wife were *so* impressed with the facilities, including the state-of-the-art birthing center with the six luxury rooms in the beautiful French country décor.

Your wife was so excited, she was telling her friends how glad she was she chose to have her baby at Jane Doe Memorial Hospital.

The only problem is that when you arrive at the hospital, every one of the luxury rooms is currently being used. The only room available is a drab room the size of a large storage closet. Your wife, who is already in labor, is beyond upset, she is crushed. She is crying, yelling, and screaming about how her baby can't be born in a room like that. Forget for a moment that people have been having babies in bushes, under trees, and in rice paddies for centuries. Unless your wife can wait for a room to open up—and if she could, you probably wouldn't be at the hospital in the first place—you may have to take whatever is available.

There really is little that you can do. As a husband, you are going to want to correct the situation and make it better, but if there is simply "no room at the inn," what can you do? The worst thing thing is to try to reason with your wife about it. She is pissed and disappointed, and there is nothing you can say or do that will change it. Don't be Mr. Fix It, and don't yell and scream at the hospital staff unless you want things to go downhill even further. Let your wife vent, rant, and rave until she gets it out of her system. In a couple of hours, she will have other things to worry about than the décor of the room.

If you do unwisely choose to rationalize with her, focus on the fact that you are soon to have a healthy baby, you are going to be parents, and that ten years from now when your kid is in Little League, nobody will remember or care the color of the room or what the picture on the wall was.

The Doctor Is an Asshole This is more common than you think. Even though your wife has her own doctor that she has visited regularly for the past eight or nine months and developed a trusting relationship with, there is an outside chance that he will not deliver your child or even see your wife during her labor and delivery. In most practices, there are several doctors who rotate on call for patients who need care after normal business hours or on weekends. If your wife delivers during a weekday or when her doctor is on call, chances are great that your wife's doctor will deliver her child. If not, don't be surprised if another doctor in the practice is the one who helps your wife and delivers the child. For most women, they at least get to meet the different doctors in the practice in the event that one of them has to deliver. But this is not the same relationship that your wife has with her own doctor.

Regardless if your wife's regular doctor or another in the practice performs the delivery, there is the small chance that he or she will simply be a jerk. Most have great bedside manners, but veteran mommies and daddies have told horror stories about doctors who will appear upset if they are called in from the golf course, late at night, or on a weekend, or of doctors who have become upset and

angry with mothers going through labor.

An extreme example of this comes from Jerry in Houston. His wife was delivering their child and was at the pushing stage. She had been pushing for quite a while, while the female doctor tried to offer encouragement. Jerry's wife ultimately became exhausted and weepy. She didn't want to push anymore. As the pregnant woman continued to cry and refuse to push, the doctor's tone changed considerably and she began to call Jerry's wife a wimp. After a few minutes of this, Jerry's wife was a complete wreck. At that point, the doctor removed her gloves and gown and told Jerry's wife, "You're wasting my time" and she proceeded to leave the room.

Jerry followed the doctor out and had a few choice words for her—but realized that he needed this doctor to perform. He managed to massage her ego enough so that she went back in with a new attitude.

Your job is not to go head to head with the doctor, but neither should you let anyone walk over your wife or ignore her wishes. Your job is to get the best performance from that doctor any way that you can, even if that means kissing a little butt. If he or she is a jerk to you or your wife, you might ask to speak with the doctor outside. Don't get into an argument or even make negative remarks in front of your wife. Handle everything behind the scenes.

The Nurses Have the Demeanor of Turkish Prison Guards By the time your child is born, you will want to adopt some of the nurses who have helped with delivery. At the very least, you will seriously consider naming your child after them. The good ones are *really* good. Some women claim that their nurses made a more memorable impact on their birth experience than the doctor.

These men and women have a difficult job. They work long hours and must deal with stressed-out, scared, clueless parents who all think that theirs is the first human child ever born. Most thoroughly enjoy their work, but like all of us they are entitled to bad days. They are, after all, human. However, we hope that their bad days are when other people are having children, not the day we show up at the hospital. If this happens and your nurse or the staff in general look as though they have just been wiped out at a Vegas black jack table, here are a few things you can do to make the most of the situation.

Empathize with the nurses and show that you know or at least understand that their job is not easy. Make simple comments and ask questions that may lighten them up, such as, "I know you must be tired, but we sure appreciate your being here to help us," "I'm sure you see a lot of rookie couples like us every day," or "What was the dumbest thing you ever saw anyone do during delivery?" Tell the staff how excited you are to have them share this experience with you. Ask your nurse personal questions. Get her talking.

Is this sucking up? Yes, it is, and most of the time it works. If it doesn't,

and you still have Cruella DeVille on your hands, then you might pull her aside, away from your wife, and explain that you understand that she sees babies being born every day and that this may be routine for her, but it is the biggest day in you and your wife's life and you would appreciate her help in keeping your spirits up and turning this into a positive situation. Be polite and sincere. I realize that you probably want to either throw up as you're saying this or give the nurse an attitude adjustment, preferably upside her head, but just as with your doctor, you want to get a great performance out of this person.

Your Wife Can't Get an Epidural in Time

"Drugs! Somebody give me drugs!" your wife is shouting. She has gone about as far as she can go on her own and can't manage the pain any more by breathing techniques. She wants, no, she *needs*, an epidural. The only problem is that your wife requested the anesthesiologist right after four other women did. It will be at least 45 minutes to an hour before she can receive her epidural. So she has to endure the pain for even longer.

But to further complicate matters, once your wife reaches a certain point in labor and is almost ready to push, they *can't* administer the epidural. So another reason she might not receive an epidural is if she becomes dilated so quickly that she misses the window of opportunity to receive it. This means that your wife will have to deliver the child as they did in the 50s—the 1850s—that is, naturally, with no drugs. She is going to give birth to something the size of a medium-sized Thanksgiving turkey. So she is likely to be feeling angry and scared. Angry because the doctor never made it there; scared, because she knows that this is really going to hurt.

Guys, there is not a lot you can do here for her except let her vent if she needs to and try to comfort her. Maybe offer a bullet to bite. Regardless, she deserves a gold medal or diamond necklace for this one.

Your Wife Must Have a Cesarean, or C-Section

Most women attempt to give birth vaginally unless there are complications that prohibit it, such as fetal distress, or if the baby is too big. Many women think of vaginal birth as *the* "birthing experience," so when after twenty-four or thirty-six hours of pushing the doctor says that in ten minutes or less he will have to perform a C-section, your wife may be crushed.

A woman many feel that a C-section robs her of the birthing experience. She may feel like a failure, or that she couldn't finish the job. The recovery for a C-section is significantly longer than that for a vaginal birth, which may also concern her. She may be upset that she will now have a long scar on her stomach and bikini season will never be the same again.

But while C-section may not be her preferred method of delivery, there is nothing wrong with it. She is not a failure or a quitter. The health of your wife and baby are paramount. You might not be able to rationalize with her or change her mind about her concerns, but you can reassure

her that she is doing the right thing for her health and for the baby. Nothing else matters.

You Miss the Birth of Your Child

One word of advice here: don't. Okay, it isn't as easy as that. Sometimes things completely beyond your control prevent you from being there. You would do anything, say anything, and pay anything to be there for your wife and your baby, but it simply can't happen. This usually happens when the baby arrives several weeks early, catching everyone by surprise.

If you are going to miss the birth and have exhausted every possible option for getting there, then you should make sure that someone is with your wife to stand in for you. She needs you, but if you can't make it, she needs to have someone. She shouldn't go through this experience by herself. Call her parents, your parents, or maybe a sibling or close friend. It doesn't matter. Have someone there for her. She will need encouragement and support. Talk to her constantly on the phone and get updates. You will feel horrible enough. Don't waste time moaning and beating yourself up about this any more than you already have. Be productive and get home as soon as you can. You might also stop at the jewelry store and the florist along the way.

■

Scott, an attorney in Des Moines, was unable to make it to the birth of his third child. This is how it happened: A year earlier, Scott's brother had

138   Daddy Smarts

become engaged. Scott was asked to serve as best man. Several months after the wedding date had been set, Scott and his wife Rhonda discovered they were pregnant.

The due date? You guessed it—the same day as the wedding. But babies are never on time, or so their doctor said. Rhonda was not able to make the trip to the wedding in Kentucky for an obvious reason, but Scott was still to go. The doctor had assured Scott and Rhonda that the baby would be late, like he had some crystal ball. Scott went to the wedding and took his two children, who were the flower girl and ring bearer.

The night after the wedding, Scott was sleeping in the hotel. In what he claims had to be an omen, his daughter, who was in the hotel bed with him, wet the bed, waking him up. Five minutes later, about 2:50 A.M., he received a phone call from his wife to inform him that she was going to the hospital, the baby was coming. Scott was facing either a seventeen-hour drive or a flight that wouldn't get him home until 1:00 P.M. the next afternoon. He was sunk. Fortunately, his wife's parents lived about an hour away from the hospital, so they were able to be with her during the entire labor and delivery. Scott was in communication with his wife the whole time. In the end, he missed the birth by about six hours. By the way, Scott and Rhonda are still happily married, so there *is* hope if you do miss the big event ... but I wouldn't chance it.

DADDY SMARTS TOP TIPS on HOSPITAL SMARTS, PART 1

- You don't ask, you don't get.
- When you arrive and get your wife settled into her room, be sure to check out where everything is.
- If you are a demanding, yelling, screaming, tyrannical jerk who berates the staff because "We called five minutes ago and nobody has come to see my wife, who is in pain, dammit!" then you and your wife will certainly be remembered. You will be remembered as that obnoxious couple who can wait until the nurses are damn good and ready.
- The best $20 investment you will ever make is in buying pizzas, bagels, Chinese food, or other take-out for the nursing staff on duty. The nurses will really appreciate it and will remember you and your wife.
- Make it a point to learn a little bit about the main nurse caring for your wife.
- If your wife is upset, focus on the fact that you are soon to have a healthy baby.
- If you can't make the birth, call her parents, your parents, or maybe a sibling or close friend. It doesn't matter. Have someone there for her.

21

What She Needs from You

About when she starts screaming, "You did this to me! You got me pregnant! It's your fault!" you may think resentfully, "Hey, maybe I've already done *enough* for you." But don't take it to heart, it's only the pain talking. Funny though, you didn't know that pain knew how to curse like that. Over the next few hours, your wife will work extremely hard, but she needs you for support and to act as her bodyguard to make sure everything goes smoothly.

Protect the QB

After your wife has been admitted and is in the labor and delivery room, it may be several hours before hard labor sets in. During this time, you may have visitors, family, and friends who want to wish you luck and to see your wife before delivery. If your wife is up for it, great. But her energy, enthusiasm, and pain will come and go very quickly. She will appear fine one moment as she is talking with people, then a contraction will hit and she will be either a zombie or doubled over in excruciating pain. It is up to you to gently herd people in or out as appropriate. Ask them to sit outside in the waiting area. You can bring them updates as things progress.

This goes for parents as well. You should talk to your spouse ahead of time to determine who she wants in the room and at what stages. She may be comfortable having her mother in the room during hard contractions, but when she starts to push, everyone except you needs to leave.

There is a lot of hubbub about the duties of a "birth coach," which sounds as if you might catch the baby between her legs like you would take a snap from center. It really is not that difficult. It is basically a title to make us feel like we are really getting in there and participating. But *valet* might be a more accurate term than *coach*.

Your Mission, Should You Choose to Accept It ...

Veteran daddies agree that your main function is to simply make your wife comfortable in any way you possibly can. She may need you to run small errands for her, such as getting ice chips or Popsicles, putting chapstick on her lips, petting her hair, or fixing her pillows. Or you may help her to manage her pain.

You can do this by using that nifty Lamaze breathing that you learned in class. Now, you may have practiced your "Super Birth Coach" technique, and are ready to cheer and count and encourage, "C'mon, baby, you can do it!" as you massage her tummy. But the fact of the matter is, while all that "rah, rah" enthusiasm sounded good in class, right now she wants you to shut up, not touch her, and just hold up your fingers so she can count. Every woman is different, but she won't really know what works until she is going through it. Follow her lead.

I Love You, Pet My Hair ... On Second Thought, Don't Touch Me, You SOB

Breathing techniques, visualization, or drugs don't matter. Face it: your wife just won't be comfortable until this baby is out of her body. She is at critical mass, and on top of that, when she is in bed and hooked up to all of the monitors, she can't move or go anywhere. If she wants to walk around the hospital or the room, she must first be detached from all the monitoring equipment. She may want to walk around the halls or visit the nursery. Some women find that the hard contractions are easier if they are standing up or if they are moving. You can offer her a shoulder

to lean on as this is going on. She may want you to help talk her through the contractions by visualizing a calm scene or a special vacation spot.

Don't be surprised if one minute she wants you near and the next minute she doesn't want you to touch her. You want to comfort her and touch her because you feel close to her. But if she snaps or asks you not to touch her, it means nothing other than that she is extremely uncomfortable. Do not get upset or have your little feelings hurt.

Spinning Heads and Pea Soup

As your wife is late in labor or pushing, she is likely to resemble Linda Blair in *The Exorcist*—complete with spinning head and speaking in a foreign language. That foreign language may actually be English, just not English as you have ever heard it come from your wife's mouth before.

Rafael, in New York, says that he was scared of the labor and delivery because he did not want to be yelled at and cursed at by his wife. Television and the movies tend to characterize women in labor as pain-crazed, out of control, and spewing venom at their husbands. Sadly, this does sometimes happen. Not always, but Rafael was there for the birth of two of his friends' children, and his buddies' wives were brutal. They were in pain and didn't know what they were saying, but it wasn't complimentary.

He was concerned that this momentous occasion would be marred by his wife's treating him like dirt, and that that is what would stick in his mind. Rafael mentioned this to his wife and she told him that she understood, but that there was no way she could tell what was going to happen during labor. "All I can do is apologize in advance." He understood but didn't like it. Fortunately for Rafael, his wife was relatively low key, and did not curse or spew pea soup.

If your wife does go off on a tirade, as hard as it may be for you, realize that she may be in uncontrollable pain. Don't listen, don't remember, and don't repeat it back to her after the baby is born. Let it drop right then.

The Waiting Game

Labor is like a series of drag races. There is a fast and furious flurry of activity followed by periods where nothing seems to be going on. Actually, there is a lot going on with your wife's body, which is doing the behind-the-scenes work in preparation for the baby.

While it may seem like downtime or that nothing is really going on, be in the moment with your wife. Do not read magazines or the newspaper and do not watch TV unless it relaxes her and she requests it. Do not make phone calls back to the office or try to get any work done. Do not pull out your laptop. And certainly don't bitch, moan, gripe, or complain about being hungry, tired, or uncomfortable. Remember that until the baby is born, your wife can't have anything

to eat or drink. She can't go to sleep. And as for comfort? C'mon.

Respect Her Decisions

Your wife may have prepared a birth plan that she has given to the doctor or nurse. It is a list of preferences, such as whether she wants drugs and if so, at what point she would like them. Even if she did not prepare a birth plan, she may have some clear ideas on what she does and doesn't want. Some couples battle over the wife's pain management choices. A few veteran daddies have had arguments with their wives in the delivery room over her choice to get an epidural or pain medication. One daddy—Randy, in Seattle—wanted his wife to hold out as long as possible before requesting her epidural, claiming that it was better for the baby. He became quite angry about it and his wife was in tears, not only because of the pain, but because her husband was a jerk.

It's Her Body

Guys, veteran daddies agree that the bottom line here is quite simple: it's her body. She knows her pain threshold. We have no business telling her what does and doesn't hurt and whether or not she needs to get the drugs if she so chooses. Just thank your lucky stars that it isn't you who has to deliver the child. Support her decisions with regard to her body. And if she begins to feel badly about requesting the pain medication or for "failing" to have a natural birth, remind her that you don't get extra

points, a gold medal, or airline miles
for being in pain. You still get to take
the baby home regardless if it hurt or
not.

- Gently and politely herd people in or
  out as appropriate.
- Determine who your wife wants in
  the room and at what stages.
- Make your wife comfortable in any
  way you possibly can.
- Every woman is different, but she
  really won't know what she needs
  from you until she is going through
  it. Follow her lead.
- Don't be surprised if one minute she
  wants you near and the next minute
  she doesn't want you to touch her. It
  means nothing other than that she is
  extremely uncomfortable. Do not get
  upset or have your little feelings
  hurt.
- If your wife does go off on a tirade,
  don't listen, don't remember, and
  don't repeat it back to her after the
  baby is born. Let it drop right then.
- Be in the moment with your wife. Do
  not read magazines or the newspaper, watch TV, make phone calls
  back to the office, or try to get any
  work done.
- Support her decisions with regard to
  her body. If she begins to feel badly
  about requesting the pain medication or for "failing" to have a natural
  birth, remind her that you don't get
  extra points, a gold medal, or airline
  miles for being in pain.

22

Hi, Daddy, I'm Your Baby

Have you noticed that on television whenever there is a birth scene, the woman has a look of exertion on her face, her hair is stylishly tousled, and she appears to be mildly sweating? She doesn't look great, but she's all right. The baby on the other hand. Wow. That is one good-looking three-month-old. Newborn babies are never that big and never that clean.

After watching plenty of birthing scenes on TV, I thought I was prepared for the moment I first saw my child. After all, on TV you see the woman's knees in the air, the edge of the blanket, the back of the doctor's head, and *voila*, out pops a fresh, sweet, and—most important—*clean* baby.

Like other rookie daddies, I was under the impression that my child would make his introduction perfectly colored and with a nice round head, happy as the baby on the Michelin Tire ads. I was ill prepared for the amount of, well, blood and junk.

("Junk" is a technical term fathers use from time to time.)

First Look

The first thing you will see is the top of your baby's head. Actually, unless your child has hair, the head will at first be tough to distinguish from your wife. When the head appears, this is called *crowning*. It will take several moments for your wife to push the remainder of the baby out. This is where the doctor plays a big part and demonstrates his skill. If the baby is too large or is at a funny angle or has an arm or shoulder in the way, the doctor must determine whether or not to perform an episiotomy, that is, to cut your wife's vagina in order to make room for the child, or to see if he can maneuver the baby into a position where it can easily come out.

In either case, as your wife continues to push, you will see more of the baby's head protrude. As the head appears, the doctor turns the baby around and you will see the face. It is still a mystery at this point whether or not you have a boy or a girl. Once the shoulders clear, the baby slides out almost effortlessly into the doctor's hands, where he will take a look at what's there and tell you that you have a baby [*insert gender of choice*].

Cutting the Cord

The baby is still attached to your wife by the umbilical cord. The doctor will place the baby on top of your wife and ask you if you would like to do the honors by cutting the cord. Veteran daddies claim that this is like setting their child free to start their life. It is a neat symbolic moment too where baby, mother, and father are all connected at once.

The doctor will hand you scissors and hold the cord for you. Don't worry about cutting the baby or your wife. The cord is very long and the doctor has sectioned off where you are supposed to cut. It cuts rather easily, with a snip and a little squirt of blood.

On a random note, how the doctor cuts the umbilical cord has nothing with determining if your child has an innie or an outie belly button. Your belly button type is determined genetically.

What Are You Feeling?

Even if you are the toughest man alive, you may cry like a baby, no pun intended. You will be in awe at how beautiful this experience is and amazed and dumbstruck that you and your wife created this thing that was not on the earth ten seconds earlier. If you are not a crier you will certainly be a screamer and shout in amaze-

ment. Not much more can be said here because words really can't describe the feeling.

Was My Child in a Fight in There?

While your child is the most beautiful sight in the world, it is a rather graphic affair. Your baby might not appear smooth and angelic like the Gerber baby. In fact, if it is a vaginal birth your child may look like a hairy cone-headed alien who has just been in a bar brawl.

A baby's fingernails can become quite long while in the womb and it is not uncommon for babies to scratch themselves before they are born. Once babies are born, nurses and parents file the nails with a very gentle emery board. But don't be surprised if your child has cuts on his face.

Babies sometimes have small pimple-like bumps on their body and face that develop in the womb. They disappear in a few days or weeks. Nothing to worry about.

Now That's My Boy

When your son is born, you may notice that his genitals seem enormous. I don't mean big for a baby, but bigger than yours. You may beam with pride, as many rookie dads do, thinking that your boy has won the genetic lottery and been, well, how shall we say … blessed.

Reality: all babies, both boys and girls, are born with swollen genitals. This is due to the hormones in your wife's body as the baby is being born. In a few hours or days, they will return to regular baby-sized genitals.

I'm Sorry, but I Ordered a Clean Baby

Sure, I saw the video during birthing class, but that was different, that was someone else. Surely *my* baby won't be covered in all that gook. Wrong. Your baby will likely be covered in fluid, blood, and a whitish, waxy substance called vernix caseosa. This is a substance that covers the baby's skin to protect it while it is being exposed to the amniotic fluid. Think of it like temporary sealer for a deck.

If your child has hair, it will be wet and matted to his head. Your baby will also have puffy eyes and wrinkled skin. Awww, it sounds so cute. Well, you wouldn't be on top of your game either, if you had just spent nine months in a small, dark, warm bathtub. Fortunately, within minutes your baby is wiped off and looking more like you think a baby should.

My Name Is Beldar Conehead and I'm from France

Because of the pressure in the birth canal, babies' heads are sometimes squeezed as they are pushed through the vagina during birth. Their skulls haven't fully fused and remain malleable for the first few weeks of their life. This means that when your baby is born, his head may have been squeezed to resemble a peanut M&M. It is not attractive. It is also not permanent.

I'm telling you, the vagina can be a rough place for babies. They not only get their head squeezed, but their entire bodies are under pressure as they pass through the birth canal. All babies are born with a bluish hue until they get oxygen. They "pink up," as it is called, in a matter of minutes after birth, and within a few hours look fine. Babies who are born via a C-section are pinker and generally do not have misshapen coneheads, because they are simply lifted out of the body and don't have to endure hours of squeezing.

Congratulations, It's a Monkey

Inside the womb, babies grow a furry hairlike covering called lanuego. This usually falls off while in the womb, but sometimes a little can remain on a baby after it is born. It will fall out in a matter of days, but it can be dark and somewhat disgusting. It kind of ruins any cute baby pictures you were hoping for. Lanuego can be anywhere on a baby's body, including the face. The night my daughter was born, there was a baby girl whose shoulders and entire forehead were covered in this thick black carpet. I'm sure she grew up to be a cute little girl, but she was born looking like a wolf child.

Once the baby is taken to the warming unit, which looks like a big heat lamp, she will be cleaned, and fluid will be sucked from her nose and mouth with a rubber bulb. She may lie naked in the tray for a few minutes, screaming.

Baby's First Test

Shortly after the baby's birth, precisely at one minute and again at five minutes, a nurse evaluates your baby's health by performing what is called an APGAR test. It's a simple method used to measure your newborn's health and to determine if he needs any emergency treatment. It evaluates:

- respiration
- heart rate
- color
- muscle tone
- reflex response

A score between zero and two is given to each area. The scores are then totaled.

While a ten is the best, most babies score between seven and ten and don't need immediate treatment, such as breathing assistance. An APGAR does not reflect future health problems, only your baby's immediate condition after birth, and is used to determine if any special treatment is necessary.

According to the medical experts at *www.babycenter.com*:

- Infants who score between eight and ten are in good to excellent condition and usually need only routine postdelivery care.
- Those who score between five and seven are in fair condition and may require some help breathing. A doctor or nurse may vigorously rub the baby's skin or place a towel with oxygen under his nose to get him to take deeper breaths.
- Infants who score under five may be in poor condition and require immediate lifesaving measures, such as an oxygen mask.

Nice Hat

Shortly after tests are performed and it is determined that the baby is out of the woods, she will be weighed, swaddled in a blanket, and given a small skull cap to prevent her from losing any heat. Babies lose most of their body heat through their heads, so it is smart to keep a hat on them. These hats are cute and look like tiny ski caps.

The nurse may place the baby back in the warming unit until mom is ready, or she may hand the child to you. When you are handed your baby, you will hold it as if it is the most fragile and precious thing on earth … and it is. The baby will be swaddled in a blanket, but you will still feel her incredible heat. Look into her eyes, study her little hands, smell her, let her hear your voice. With my daughter, I was the first to hold her and it was the most wonderful experience of my life. I stared into these enormous dark almond-shaped eyes and knew, after only a few minutes of her being alive that I was in love.

How Do I Hold Him?

You may be excited and thrilled at the prospect of holding your child but simultaneously scared to death. Why? Quite simply, she is small, fragile, and precious. You regularly purchase grocery items that are larger than your child. Unless you have held a baby before, you, like many men, may be fearful of dropping the child or harming it somehow.

Rookie fathers end up erring on

the side of caution, but that it is okay. You aren't going to harm, break, drop, or damage your child. You will get the hang of it eventually. Babies, while fragile in many respects, are much tougher than you think. Watch how the nurses and the doctor handle the child.

You can cradle her like a football in the crook of your arm, or you can hold her close to your chest with her head near your shoulder. The thing that you need to remember is to be very mindful of your baby's neck and head. Her neck muscles can't support the weight of her head and won't be able to for quite some time. Be sure when you are holding the baby that you support her head and neck.

Take Photos

Video is fine, but make sure you take some still photos of the baby. These will become treasures. Also, when your baby is lying swaddled in the warming unit waiting to be held for the first time, make sure that you get some tight pictures of her face.

If you have a digital camera, you can even post these on the Web or e-mail them to friends and family who couldn't be there with you.

Mom Still Has Work to Do

While your baby is being cleaned off, weighed, and wrapped up, your wife actually has some more pushing to do. Even though the baby is out, the placenta, which helps sustain your baby throughout pregnancy, is still in there. With several more pushes, the placenta will exit and the doctor will inspect it to make sure that it is intact and that nothing remains inside of your wife. If the placenta falls apart and pieces are left inside of your wife, she can develop a serious infection and complications. The doctor may ask you if you want to see it before he disposes of it. It's your call. If you think you might be fascinated by what looks like an enormous slab of liver, go right ahead. I passed.

After the placenta is removed, the doctor will spend a few more minutes attending to your wife, repairing any vaginal tears or cuts that were a result of the birth. If your wife was fortunate enough not to tear or require an episiotomy, great. Her recovery will be that much quicker and less painful. If she tore or was cut, then she will need stitches. It may be that she needs only two or three, or she may need significantly more. She is most likely drugged and can't feel what is going on. Despite the cuts or tears, everything will be back to normal in a few weeks.

Do yourself a favor and don't watch this procedure. You have a beautiful new baby to look at, and watching a doctor sew up your wife's vagina is not on any husband's top ten list.

Once the doctor is finished, you can bring baby to mother. The three of you will want to spend a few moments together before you go outside and spread the news.

DADDY SMARTS TOP TIPS on
MEETING YOUR BABY

- Newborn babies are never as big and clean as they appear on TV.
- If given the chance, cut the cord. It is an amazing experience.
- How the doctor cuts the umbilical cord has nothing with determining if your child has an innie or an outie belly button. Your belly button is determined genetically.
- No matter how tough you are, you will cry like a baby when you see your child for the first time.
- Your baby might not appear smooth and angelic like the Gerber baby. In fact, if born vaginally, your child may look like a hairy coneheaded alien who has just been in a bar brawl.
- All vaginally-born babies have a bluish hue until they get oxygen. They "pink up," as it is called, in a matter of minutes, and within a few hours look fine.
- Babies who are born via C-section are pinker and generally do not have misshapen coneheads because they are simply lifted out of the body and don't have to endure hours of squeezing.

- Rookie fathers err on the side of caution, but that is okay. You aren't going to harm, break, drop, or damage your child. Watch how the nurses and the doctor handle the child.
- Be sure that when you are holding the baby you support her head and neck. Her neck muscles can't support the weight of her head, and won't be able to for quite some time.
- Video is fine, but make sure you take some still photos of the baby.

23

Spreading the News and Settling In

This is your moment—Dad. Hey, that handle sounds pretty good. You are ready to leave the delivery room to tell others your twosome now numbers three. As you walk or run down that hallway, take a second to remember everything, because you are about to deliver news that changes people's lives.

If you have friends or family in the waiting room, go out and tell them directly. Some guys just blurt it out and run back. Others stay for a little while and get hugs all around. My buddy Steve actually taped the family's reaction as he told everyone about the birth of his daughter. You can say, "We would like to welcome Grace Renee Smith to the world," or you can simply say, "It's a girl." Or you can come up with some creative way to share the news, but you will likely come unglued when the big moment comes. That's all right because it's an exciting and joyous moment. When you deliver the news, be sure to tell the baby's weight if you

know it, and give an update on the mom's condition. Let them know that they will be able to come in to see mom and baby in a few moments.

It might be thirty minutes or more after the baby is born until visitors are allowed to come in and see Mommy and the new baby. So your guests have some cooling-down time between when you announce you're a Dad and actually getting to hold the baby.

Can I Hold Her?

This is a huge deal and must be played carefully. There is a certain pecking order that must be followed or you run the risk of starting a full-scale family feud. Regardless of who else is there, grandparents are first. No questions asked. If neither set of grandparents is present, it isn't as tough.

The order is as follows: grandparents, aunts and uncles, other family members, closest friends. The main ones to remember here are of course the grandparents and aunts and uncles. If one set of grandparents is at the hospital, there is no problem or question. But if both your wife's parents and yours are there, you should probably defer to her parents first. You and your wife can discuss this pecking order before the baby is born so there is no confusion on Labor Day.

You and your wife may choose differently and that is fine. What you want to avoid is a scene where *other* people are choosing who holds the baby. If you and your wife decided on an order of who will hold the child, then it is up to you, Dad, to follow it, placing the child in the arms of whomever you wish to be next. Otherwise, it can become a mad baby grab.

He Looks Like *Our* Side of the Family

Be prepared for an onslaught of instant critiques. Everyone is suddenly a genetic engineer and expert on whom this child favors. "Oh, he looks like you as a baby. That is our nose. Yeah, he sure got your eyes. Oh, that is Aunt Ethyl's mouth." Just let them rant. All new babies look like little blue or pink M&Ms wrapped in a blanket, so nobody can really tell anything for a few days.

Now might be a good time to announce your child's name to the world. If the name was chosen to honor someone, telling the name in the waiting room can be a very special way of introducing the baby to that person or honoring a person's memory. "We would like to introduce

Billy Bob Jones. We named him after *you*, Daddy."

Once you have made the big announcement to the friends, family, and well-wishers who may have joined you at the hospital, it is on to telling the rest of the world about your news.

Chances are pretty good that your wife has made a "call list" of special people who couldn't be there but whom you wish to tell immediately that the baby has been born. You can call the people you are closest to, but as for the rest, it is best to hand this list to a friend or family member. They will want to tell just the facts: boy or girl, the name, and weight if possible.

Smart Stuff to Remember

A great way to share the news and answer everyone's questions is to change the outbound message on your home voice mail to announce the pertinent details. "Hello, you have reached the new and improved Anderson family. Joyce gave birth to a little girl named Grace Louise at 2:37 A.M. Tuesday. Grace is 7.2 pounds and 19 inches. Mom, Grace, and Dad are fine. We are at Methodist Hospital, Room 345."

The Push Gift

Now that the baby is here, we can take a moment to check the score. If you are keeping a running tally at home of what your wife has gone through versus what you have gone through from conception through delivery, this is the way our judges core it.

She gained over 30 pounds and had her whole body become an uncomfortable and unfamiliar pod for over nine months so a creature the size of a football could take twenty-four to thirty-six hours to come out of her body through a hole normally only a few inches in diameter.

You got to have plenty of amazing sex. You also endured your longest dry spell since junior high. You lost some hair and sleep worrying about money, your baby, your life, and your wife. You had to put up with a lot of stupid questions from well-intentioned strangers. You had to carry a lot of bags. You had to put some stuff together around the house, despite the fact that you aren't very handy. You had to endure an earful of bitching from time to time. You had to drive to the hospital and watch. You had to count and say "Breathe, baby, breathe."

Okay, judges? What do you say? Veteran daddies have to give it to the ladies. They have soundly kicked our butts and proven to us once again that if it were left to men to become pregnant, humans would become extinct. For the record, the Russian judge took away points for bad form during the sixth month.

You and your wife have given each other the greatest gift in the world, a healthy beautiful little baby, and have turned your twosome into a three-some—or something even larger. You owe each other nothing but love.

However, veteran daddies highly recommend, let me repeat this, *highly* recommend that you produce some small token or bauble as a gesture of appreciation for your wife and her valiant efforts in delivery. Oh, let's just cut the crap, shall we? Go buy her some jewelry. Veteran mommies across the board say that coughing up jewelry and flowers shortly after birth is a widely acceptable way for daddies to say, "Thank God it was you, not me, who had to go through that."

Jewelry works because she will always remember the birth of your kids when she wears it. Stay away from rings because her fingers will still be swollen. Earrings, necklaces, and bracelets work well. You don't have to spend a lot of money. A real neat and fairly inexpensive jewelry item is a charm bracelet with mommy charms or little kids on it.

When the drugs and euphoria wear off, she will not only feel like a truck has hit her … she will look like it too. Not to say she will look *bad*, but she will look exhausted, and having something nice and new to wear will make her feel pretty. Plus, she will show it to her friends and family and your stock will again hit a new fifty-two-week high as the big dog stud husband on the block.

You should give your gift to her a couple of hours after the baby is born when she gets settled in her room. You can take it to the hospital with you, but be careful. It is a crazy, chaotic time and you certainly don't want to run the risk of losing it. The best thing is to leave it with your parents, in-laws, or a friend who will be there after the baby is born. Try to purchase something several weeks before the baby is due so you aren't caught by surprise, or worse, empty-handed.

The First Night as Mom and Dad

About an hour after the family and well-wishers have gone home, the baby is safe in the nursery having some routine tests run and your wife is checked into her room. Things finally seem to have calmed down. You are both thoroughly exhausted, but wired and excited too. You finally look at each other sitting in the silence and you just breathe a sigh of relief. You've made it. This is your first night as parents. Now for two simple but important decisions. Where do you and the baby sleep?

Many hospitals give you the choice to have the baby sleep in the same room as your wife. Mom may still be so incredibly attached to the baby that she doesn't want to let him go and wants to keep him in sight. She also might want to try to breast-feed him throughout the night and would like to have him readily available. All are very valid reasons. If your wife chooses to keep the baby in her room, fine. Many first-time parents want to keep the baby in the room with Mom.

However, veteran mommies and daddies ask you to consider letting the baby sleep in the nursery for the first night. Your wife will be completely worn out and need her rest. The last thing she needs is a screaming baby next to her all night long.

What role do you play in all of this? It is up to you to do what is best

for your wife right now. If you have to be the heavy and tell her to get some rest, then do it. If you choose to keep the baby in the room with you, you will find yourself constantly peeking at the baby and just staring. You will be in awe that this is your child and that just a few hours ago he was not here on earth. It's pretty heady stuff. But your watching that peaceful little sleeping sweetie assumes that sweetie is sleeping. If your child is not sleeping and isn't in the nursery, then you will get a crash course in how to feed or comfort a child.

Where Will You Sleep?

Go home. You can't do anything else. You need to clean up. There is nowhere for you to sleep anyway. If you don't, you will get absolutely no decent sleep and you will be a wreck for the next couple of days as you greet visitors.

Listen to the voice of experience. With our first child, I stayed in the room with my wife and baby. My wife was thoroughly worn out and her boobs felt as though they were about to explode, not to mention what the rest of her felt like. I pushed two standard-issue hospital guest chairs circa 1970 together to make a crude bed that constantly came apart, sending my butt to the floor. And in the plastic baby bed next to us lay six-hour-old Samantha, who used her new lungs to scream constantly for three hours straight.

Meredith and I each clumsily tried to calm the baby. Meredith, whose breast-feeding experience was zip, tried unsuccessfully to get Samantha to latch on to her breast. (Guys, it is not as easy for a baby to grab a boob as you might think.) She was in pain and tears were streaming down her face. "I'm a bad mother. I can't feed my baby." I was starting to get upset because I was about as useful as a bump on a log. There was a three-hour stretch when we were looking for the receipt so we could return the kid and get our money back. We were complete wrecks until we finally threw in the towel and called for the nurse to take the baby to the nursery.

With baby number two, we learned from our experience. We kept him in the room only for a little while before calling that wonderful nurse to take our son to the nursery, where trained professionals could attend to his every little need and could bring him back to us in moments with one call. The drugs were beginning to wear off my wife and she wanted to sleep, so I kissed her good night, told her I loved her, and got in my car to go home where I slept, well, like a baby. When I arrived at the hospital the next morning at 7:30, my wife was up and had showered, and the nurse had just brought my son in ten minutes earlier. Everyone was happy, rested, and refreshed. Life was good.

When it is time for both you and your wife to get sleep, take full advantage of having a nurse who can keep the baby with her throughout the night. In two days, when you get home, you are on your own. You will not have more than three hours of continuous sleep for several weeks, if not months. Worn out and stressed

out is not a great way to start your parenting adventure. Go home, get some rest, and return to the hospital early the next morning.

DADDY SMARTS TOP TIPS on SPREADING THE NEWS AND SETTLING IN

- Be sure to tell the weight if you know it, and give an update on mom's condition. Let visitors know that they will be able to come in to see mom and baby in a few moments.
- It might be thirty minutes or more after the baby is born before visitors are allowed to come in and see Mommy and the new baby.
- Regardless of who else is there, grandparents are the first people to hold the child after the parents.
- Be prepared for an onslaught of instant critiques. Everyone is suddenly a genetic engineer and expert on whom this child favors.
- Change the outbound message on your home voice mail to announce the baby and pertinent details.
- Purchase some small token or bauble as a gesture of appreciation for your wife and her valiant efforts in delivery. Hint: jewelry.
- Your wife will check into her room around an hour or two after having the baby.
- Consider letting the baby sleep in the nursery for the first night. Your wife will be completely worn out and will need her rest.
- It is up to you to do what is best for your wife right now. If you have to be

the heavy and tell her to get some rest, then do it.

- Go home. You can't do anything else. If you don't, you will get no decent sleep and you will be a wreck for th next couple of days as you greet visitors.

24

Hospital Smarts, Part 2

Earlier I gave you the scoop on how to get the best service and performance from the labor and delivery staff. I'm sure that you charmed them all and they treated you as if you were the first couple to have ever given birth. Right? I hope you remember what worked because it will come in handy again now that your wife has moved to her room, which is likely on a different floor and certainly staffed by a different crew of nurses.

Not much is different here except that you should make it a point to personally go out to the desk and meet the people working that shift. Do this for the morning and evening shifts. Be especially friendly to the person behind the desk who answers the calls from patients' rooms. He or she will determine whether or not your wife gets her pain medication now or sometime next year.

And the Mr. Congeniality Award Goes to ...

Be personable with everyone who comes in contact with your wife. Say good morning and good night. If something doesn't go right or if someone is slow to respond, you should go out and talk to someone at the desk rather than screaming on the intercom. If you know their name it can be more effective to say, "Hi, Renee, this is Bradley—Meredith is really in a lot of pain, and she wanted me to ask you if we could...." than to scream on the intercom, "My wife needs some Tylenol! Can somebody please come down here?" It is common sense and common courtesy, but it can go a long way.

Remember how I recommended winning nurses' hearts through their stomachs? This wisdom also applies to the nurses caring for your wife after the baby is born. When you come back in the morning to see your wife and baby, bring a dozen or so donuts or bagels with cream cheese and drop them off at the nurse's station with a card that says, "Thanks for your help. We appreciate it." Sign it from you, your wife, and the baby and don't forget your room number.

If you want to deliver the breakfast items, candy, cookies, or pizza in person, it is helpful to do it when there are a lot of nurses and staff around the desk so you get maximum exposure. Introduce yourself and mention your wife's name along with the room number. "Hi, I'm George Jetson. My wife, Jane, is in room 333A. We would just like to thank you all for your help with everything. Our boy Elroy is doing great. Thanks for making this a great experience and taking such good care of Jane. These are for you. Enjoy." Is this cheesy? You're darn right it is. And it works like a charm. Do this for both the morning and evening shifts, and you will find it is one of the best twenty-dollar investments in the world.

The nursery staff, which takes care of your baby, deserves some attention too. Introduce yourself so they can start to recognize you and your child. It is tougher to schmooze them and tougher to feed them, too, because you have less contact with them than the other staff. Still, it always helps to be friendly when picking up your child or dealing with any of the hospital staff.

Now that the baby is born, there is both good news and not-so-good news. For the past nine months, all attention has been focused solely on your wife, the expectant mother. She has been in the spotlight front and center and you have been relegated to what seemed like a chorus part. The good news is that she is no longer the center of attention. The not-so-good news is that neither are you. In fact, you just got moved to third string.

You've Been Benched

I say this jokingly, but it really can sting a little bit. Shortly after my daughter was born, a close friend came to visit us at the hospital. We had several people in the room and she took a picture of me with my child. She said, "Enjoy it. This will be the last picture you will ever be in, Daddy." I asked what she meant and she told me that daddies always take the pictures, so they are never in them. I was pissed. This person had several kids and maybe her husband wasn't in any pictures but I'd be damned, I thought, if I was going to be pushed right out. But in fact many daddies do take a back seat as soon as the child is born.

Sure, there is some congratulatory back slapping from well-wishers, but people quickly lose interest in you. They only want to hear Mom's version of the events and then demand, "Now hand me that sweet little baby." Get used to it, it only gets worse. What is funny is that about two or three months from now, when your own parents come to visit, even *they* don't care to see you. You will open the door and they walk right past you, saying, "Oh, hi, now where's my little grandbaby?"

Are You Prepared for Opening Day?

Let's say you have gone home to shower and rest. You are probably still exhausted, but excited too. Now that everything has happened and the baby is here, what do you do? You prepare for the onslaught of visitors. Hopefully people will call before they come to the hospital. If so, you should tell them when you would like visitors. Although the hospital's visiting hours may be all day, you should work in some downtime and plan for a few hours where there are no visitors. This way you and your wife and baby can spend some time getting used to one another. Your wife can rest or practice feeding the baby.

Your wife's recovery is the priority. People can always come by the house later in the week to see the baby, and in fact it is okay if you allow only family to come to the hospital. If it appears that your wife is getting tired or overwhelmed, it is up to you to politely usher people out. Thank them for coming and apologize, but let them know that your wife needs her rest. I can't stress enough how important it is for her to rest while in the hospital where someone can take care of her.

This Isn't a Cafeteria

When you have visitors, ask them politely not to bring in food from the outside and eat it in the room. Hospital rooms are small and the smells can linger. If someone brings in McDonald's and leaves the bag, your wife's

room will smell like french fries for two days. Unless your wife requests it, leave outside food outside.

Can You Cover Your Mouth When You Cough?

Don't let people bring their kids if they are sick or have just gotten over an illness. Also, if kids are wild, dirty, or out of control, have them wait outside. Don't count on other parents to discipline their kids in this situation. You set the terms for your baby.

Sickness applies to everyone, not just kids. If an adult has a cold, virus, or other bug, it is best that they don't hold the baby. This can be really tough, but it is in the baby's best interest and hopefully they will understand. Babies' immune systems aren't fully developed yet and they are very susceptible to infections, colds, and germs. Just to be safe, make everyone wash his or her hands before holding the baby.

Don't Hoard the Baby

Let others hold the child. By the same token, don't let one individual hoard the baby. You have to be the referee and determine who holds and for how long.

Orlando, a veteran daddy in Miami, had a problem because his wife refused to let anyone other than herself and her husband hold the baby, including her own parents and her in-laws. She wouldn't let the grandparents hold the baby for a week, because she "didn't trust them." Never mind that her parents managed to raise *her* without dropping her on her head—or maybe they did, and this was the result.

Will, a retail manager in Baltimore, tells of a great-aunt who visited the hospital and became so attached to his baby son that she sat in the chair rocking and holding the child for over an hour before giving him to anyone else.

If someone is unfamiliar with holding a baby, you should instruct him to support the baby's head—like *you* are this big professional now. You might even have people sit in a certain chair. You can hand them the baby and take her back when they want to get up.

Everyone will want to have their picture with the baby. Have a separate disposable camera and take at least one picture of each visitor holding the baby. You can send it to them in a few weeks.

Be Nice

Chances are that you still might be exhausted and feel that everyone has seen the baby but you. Don't let yourself be pushed out of the way or pulled in too many directions. This is a special time for you, your wife, your new family. Do what is right for you during this time—but don't rip people's heads off, either.

DADDY SMARTS TOP TIPS on
HOSPITAL SMARTS, PART 2

- Go to the desk and meet the people working that shift.
- Be personable with everyone who comes in contact with your wife.
- Nurses + Food = Success
- Work in some downtime with no visitors so you and your wife and baby can spend some time getting used to one another.
- If it appears that your wife is getting tired or overwhelmed, it is up to you to politely usher people out.
- Don't let people bring their kids if they are sick or have just gotten over an illness. If an adult has a cold, virus, or other bug, it is best that they don't hold the baby.
- Make everyone washes his or her hands before holding the baby.
- Have a separate disposable camera and take at least one picture of each visitor as they are holding the baby. You can send it to them in a few weeks.
- Don't let yourself be pushed out of the way or pulled in too many directions.

25

Going Home

t is time to go home. And although the last couple of days have been a whirlwind, by next week you will look back on them much like you do a vacation long after you get home. "That was nice, but it wasn't long enough." You have tried your best to talk the nurses into moving in with you, but to no avail.

You are excited, but you also feel like a man who is about to walk the plank and be dropped into the vast ocean of parenthood without a life vest. At home it is you and your wife against a much smaller but crafty and unpredictable opponent. There are no nurses around to tell you what to do, no call buttons so someone can take your crying baby back to the nursery and let you get a full night's sleep. You are about to graduate to full-time parenting.

When Should We Go Home?

If your insurance is paying for two days, then by all means take the two days. It is paid for and doesn't cost you a thing. No matter how great your wife feels, talk her into staying so she can at least rest for one more night.

According to your insurance company, the meter starts running the moment your wife checks into her hospital room, not during the labor and delivery. This means that if, after the birth, your wife checks into her room at 8:30 P.M., you have until 8:30 P.M. two days from then before you have to check out. It isn't like a hotel, where you have to leave by noon. You usually get your whole forty-eight hours. Veteran daddies say that you should check out as late in the day as possible to take full advantage of the nursing care for your wife and baby.

Take Everything—You've Paid for It

Have you ever rolled your eyes because your mother seems to take everything that isn't nailed down in a hotel room? Every knickknack, tchotchke, toiletry item, and give-away is stuffed into her purse. "Hey, you never know when you might need it," she replies. One friend's mother-in-law has a drawer full of soy sauce and ketchup packets from fast-food restaurants and Chinese takeout. It is like she is hoarding things for the Apocalypse.

As embarrassing as that kleptomaniacal habit may be, when it comes to hospitals, Mom may be on to something. Veteran mommies and daddies claim that there are so many goodies to take home that it makes taking a few soaps from the Holiday Inn look tame. However, don't think you are getting all of these amenities for free. If you snag a shampoo bottle or a few of those cute miniature soaps from a hotel, you usually don't find them on your bill at one hundred times their normal cost.

Everything that your wife has used, touched, or seen in that room is being tacked on your bill, and you can bet that the prices are a few hundred, if not thousand, percent more than you would expect to pay at your local Target or Wal-Mart. You know that little box of tissues by your wife's bed? That's about five dollars, so take it. They're made of gold. The night you checked into the room, your wife was given a giant seventy-two-ounce plastic mug with a straw. Take that too. That probably cost more than a month's worth of double lattes at Starbucks.

Take any extra diapers, wipes, and baby caps, as well as pads for your wife and as many pairs of that fishnet underwear as you can. This sounds cheap, and maybe it is, but you are paying for it.

Honey, Don't Forget Your Fishnet Underwear

I knew I got your attention with the fishnet underwear. Cool it down there, chief. I know it has been a while, but trust me, these are not some sexy little Victoria's Secret thing that you might see a supermodel wearing in the catalog. You know the trauma your wife's genitalia have endured in the past few days, especially if she has had an episiotomy. There is still much healing to be done, and it is often difficult for women to put on regular panties for a few days. There can still be bleeding for several days after birth. So hospitals provide women with what look like maxipads for giants. They are enormous. Since there are no tabs or tape to hold them in place, the hospitals have these huge net panties which fit loosely yet hold the pad in place. These are purely a matter of function over form. She may still be uncomfortable for a few days, so take some home. And don't count on her wearing these around the house no matter how much you beg.

Blue Bulb Suckers

Obviously not the technical name for them—they are called "aspirators"—but take as many of these as you can get your hands on. You might even ask the nurse for one or two extra if you've schmoozed her correctly. These are the rubber bulbs that the doctors and nurses use to suck mucus and fluid from the baby's nose. Babies can't blow their noses and won't even be able to try for at least a year to a year and a half. If your baby is stopped up, which there is a good chance he will be sometimes because babies' nasal passages are so small, these are the only things that work. You can buy something like them at the drug store, but they are not as small or effective as the ones you get from the hospital.

Car Seats and a Clean House

You're a prepared dad and have already put the car seat in, right? Good man. If not, go do it now. Remember that car seats always go in the back seat and face the rear of the car. Uh, you *bought* the car seat already, didn't you?

Will your baby have a place to sleep when you get home? If you haven't already prepared everything, you need to make sure that the furniture is delivered and assembled before you get home.

The worst thing is coming home to a disaster area with dirty clothes on the floor and dishes in the sink. I'm certainly not a clean freak—ask my wife—but you are making a fresh start and have a lot of work cut out for you in the next few days as you become a family. Clean up the house before your family comes home or ask a family member or friend to help. Or pay for a maid service to come in. It is worth the money.

Paperwork

Most hospitals today take care of the paperwork necessary for your child to receive a birth certificate. You complete the forms before you leave the hospital and you receive the certificate in a few weeks. If you aren't approached about this, be sure to ask what steps you need to take. It can vary from state to state.

The moment of truth is when the bill arrives. You may have welled up a little and formed a tear when your child was born, but you will cry your eyes out when the bill comes. Actually, as I explained earlier in the book, your insurance will take care of the lion's share of the expenses. However, depending on complications, you could still be looking at a minimum of several hundred to a couple of thousand dollars. The morning that you and your family are to check out, someone from accounting will drop by to go over the bill with you and explain the charges. You can discuss payment options and plans at that time. Remember, many hospitals now take credit cards, if that is easier for you.

There might be a little financial anxiety on your part. If it makes you feel any better, have this discussion outside of the room, away from your wife. I'm not saying this to imply in any way that finances are a man's thing. No way. But if money is a concern and something that both of you worry about, there is no need to take away from this day by having both of you drive home stunned at how much it all cost. Let this be her day. Take care of it now, discuss it in a day or two.

Lights, Camera, Action

You want to remember everything about this day, so take plenty of pictures and video. Before you clear the hospital room out, take still photos of each floral arrangement and then video the room.

Your wife has likely picked out a "going home" out fit for baby. Lay a pretty blanket flat on the bed and place your baby on it. It will serve as a nice backdrop for you to take pictures of your child before she goes home. You and your wife should surround the baby and have someone take plenty of pictures and video of the three of you.

Be sure to get several still shots as well as video of mom and baby being wheeled out of the hospital. This is one for the scrapbook. Don't forget to get *in* some pictures, too. You're a dad, not Ansel Adams, so ask a nurse or a stranger to film or take pictures.

The Ride

If you could, you would paint "Caution! Precious Cargo" on the side of your car. Never in your life will you drive so safely, so slowly, and so cautiously. You will be looking at the other cars speeding by and wonder what the hurry is. "They should be more careful." Where a yellow light once meant "punch it," it now means "stop." You will lighten up in a few weeks, but for now being "safety man" is your job.

I can't stress this enough. Your baby must *always* be placed in the back seat in a rear-facing car seat. For this first ride or two, your wife might want to sit in the back with the baby. However, this isn't necessary and certainly is not required long term. Jonathan, an insurance executive in Atlanta, says, "My wife was fanatical about riding in the back. For three months I felt like a chauffeur."

Make a "Welcome Home" Sign

This makes your wife feel special and will make for great photos. You can make a banner on your computer, or you can purchase a decorative flag that says "It's a Boy" or "New Arrival." These can be purchased for around twenty dollars at a local arts and crafts store or gift shop. In some areas, you can rent a large wooden cutout of a stork carrying a baby, which you can put in your yard. They come in pink or blue and have an area where your baby's name and birth info are painted on. Prices vary around the country from $50 to $100 for the week. Ask someone at your local Babies R Us registry or maternity shop if they know whom to contact in your area.

Welcome Home

This will be as momentous as when you carried your wife over the threshold. When you park the car, have your wife and baby wait a second so you can film it. Better yet, have someone else meet you to film your arrival.

For the first day back home, try not

to have company, or at least keep it to a minimum. You two will still need to rest, and those few hours right after bringing your child home are precious. You are starting to set the tone for your family life and getting used to each other. You have taken the long journey and survived the many challenges. You are no longer a rookie … at least where pregnancy is concerned. But there is a lot left to learn and experience. Now it is time to move to the next stage of fatherhood, Life After Baby.

DADDY SMARTS TOP TIPS **on GOING HOME**

- If your insurance is paying for two days, take two days. It is paid for and doesn't cost you a thing.
- Check out as late in the day as possible to take full advantage of the nursing care for your wife and baby.
- Take everything. You've paid for it.
- Clean up the house before your family comes home or ask a family member or friend to help you straighten things up.
- Many hospitals now take credit cards.

- Don't forget to get *in* some pictures, too. You're a dad, not Ansel Adams, so ask a nurse or a stranger to videotape or take pictures.
- Make a "Welcome Home" sign.
- For the first day back home, try not to have company, or at least keep it to a minimum. You two will still need to rest, and those few hours right after bringing your child home are precious.

Life A.B.—
After Baby

*If you thought your life has under-
gone some changes over the past
nine months, you ain't seen nothing yet.*

*This section helps you adjust to
your new life, family, and responsibilities as some things change and
others return to normal—or as normal as they can be for a rookie
father.*

Welcome to the club, Daddy.

26

The First Few Days

One night you are a couple, the next you are a three-some. Instant family. Just add water and love, batteries sold separately. You've had a couple of days at the hospital to get used to things, but that really doesn't prepare you for life once you are home.

There has been so much excitement and activity swirling around you in preparation for the baby that you would think things might slow down now that the baby is here. Wrong. The party is just getting started. I warn you, your life will be in fifth gear for about the next, say, eighteen years. You will face many trying times as a parent, but few will be as challenging as the first few days in your new role. There is plenty of activity in and around the house, but not everyone will be feeling or operating at 100 percent.

She Is in Pain ... Still

For starters, your wife is likely to still be in some pain. Depending on her condition after birth, she may still not be very mobile and may still be experiencing bleeding, particularly if she required stitches. If she experienced a C-section, she might even be in bed and certainly won't be able to lift anything over a few pounds.

Regardless of the type of birth or her condition, her throbbing breasts are likely to hurt so badly that they will take her mind off of any other pain. If her milk has not already come in while you were at the hospital then it surely will start shortly after arriving home.

You both will be exhausted and beaten. Even if your wife was able to get some rest in the hospital, her body has been through a traumatic experience. She will likely be at less than full speed for a week or so at the very least. You too will be tired and worn out from the excitement, running around, preparing for the baby, and caring for your wife. You may also be pulling double or triple duty between helping with the new baby, keeping up your regular job (if you failed to take time off from work), and serving as tour guide and host for any out-of-town visitors and guests who came to see the baby.

Becoming a Family

At least for the first day or two, try to limit the number of visitors and activities around your house. You certainly want to invite people over to see the child and to wish you and your wife congratulations, but this is a precious time that will only happen once. Don't let the awe of it all pass you by. The three of you need some time to get used to one another. Block out a few uninterrupted hours for your new family to be home alone. Put the baby in her bassinet and just watch her and each other. Take turns holding her. Give her a tour of your house and her new room. This will be the start of your bonding experience.

Encourage Visitors, but Make It on Your Terms

Once you are home and have settled in, you can expect the onslaught of visitors and well-wishers. Understand that people will come to see you, but they aren't coming to see *you*. They want to see and hold the baby and hear mom's birthing story.

To prevent your home from becoming Grand Central Station at rush hour, you should establish set visiting hours, just like the hospital. Schedule two big blocks of time each day when people can drop by unannounced. You may feel a little formal doing this, but otherwise you are likely to have a constant barrage of people and you will remain exhausted or you won't get any family time. Tell people who call when you would prefer for guests to come by. You can also record the times you prefer to have visitors on your answering machine. This way, people know when it is okay to come by and they can just drop in when you are expecting visitors.

Create your visiting hours so that they work around Mom's schedule. Give her plenty of time to take naps, clean up, and feed the baby. And don't be afraid to reschedule visits if your wife or the baby aren't feeling well. A rough night with a crying baby gives you the right to change the schedule at your discretion.

Take Some Time Off

This is a rare and special time that you will never be able to recreate. If you are able, take a few days off from work. Plan for it to be a long weekend at the very least. If you are so vital to your organization that the free market system will crash if you fail to show up for work, then bring work home, telecommute, or pass the responsibility to someone else for a few days. For the first week or so, your mind won't be on work regardless of what you do. Your family needs you, and you will need them.

Bring in Some Help

To help you and your wife adjust to life with a newborn and catch up on your rest, you might consider hiring a temporary live-in nanny or nurse for the first few days or weeks. Sometimes referred to as a "night nurse," such a person can help you and your wife manage the transition from hospital to home.

The night nurse will often take care of the baby in the middle of the night so mom can rest. She may feed the baby through a bottle with pumped or expressed milk (breast milk extracted from a mechanical breast pump or manually squeezed out by your wife) or bring the baby to mom. She may try to get your baby on a sleeping schedule, for which she would deserve a medal or a new car. Fees and services provided can vary widely. Have your wife talk with her doctor's office to learn of agencies or people who provide these services.

You don't have to have a live-in nanny or nurse. Many couples hire someone to help with the baby during the day or to assist with light cleaning and housekeeping while mom gets her strength back.

Some couples choose to have a mother or mother-in-law stay to help as nurse. As I've said before, when I got married, I hit the in-law lotto. If the worst thing I have to do is answer a few questions and carry a box or two in from the car, then I'm a lucky man. My mother in-law was an invaluable help during the early days. She came in to town for about two weeks to help cook, clean, shop, and take care of the baby so my wife could rest. She went above and beyond the call of duty. Now hear this. She came in to town for two weeks; she did not stay with us for two weeks. She stayed with friends or at a hotel. She came over early in the morning and stayed until after dinner or when the baby was down for a brief evening nap. I was back at work in a week, so it didn't matter to me if she was around all day. At the end of the day, everyone was happy and our little family was still able to have some time alone.

Uh, Mom, It's Not *Your* Baby

Some veteran dads warn of potential friction between your wife and her mother. Mothering doesn't always come naturally to every woman. Just because someone has breasts and gives birth doesn't mean that she is good at it from day one. If your mother-in-law is a dominant type that needs to be the center of attention, she may inadvertently steal the spotlight from your wife and run over her feelings by trying to "outmother" the new mom. You will quickly know if your mother-in-law (or mother) is doing this because she will try to constantly correct your wife or criticize her parenting skills. She may even go so far as to prevent your wife from holding the baby or caring for the child. It is a classic case of a teacher growing impatient with a student and finally saying, "Here is how you do this. Oh, just let me show you instead."

Why does this matter to you? Because after about two days of it, your wife will want to scream. She is just learning to be a mother, which is not easy, and she may feel like a failure. If her own mother is reinforcing this, by accident or not, your wife might slip into post partum depression, and you do not want or need that.

Your job is to support your wife and to play traffic cop. Ultimately, it is something that must be discussed between mother and daughter. But you can make sure that you positively reinforce your wife's behavior with the baby and make sure that your mother-in-law, aunt, friend, or who-ever does not monopolize the baby and squeeze your wife out. I need to mention that if it is your own mom doing the correcting, then there is a serious problem. You should pull Mom aside, thank her for the help, let her know how much you appreciate her, but gently let her know that she needs to give your wife some space.

Realize that I'm not talking about overzealous helping, but about some-one taking the focus and joy away from your wife. Your job as protector doesn't end once you leave the hos-pital.

Sorry, No Room at the Inn

If you are fortunate enough to have relatives who can be with you to help after the baby is born, then count your blessings. But just because you have family available to help doesn't mean that family should stay with you.

Don't underestimate how stressful having a new baby in the house can be, especially for rookies. You and your wife will not always know what to do and can be overwhelmed. Add to that the additional pressures of having family and in-laws under the same roof and you can have a recipe for disaster.

If you are trying to choose whether or not to have family stay with you at your home, veteran daddies offer this simple advice ... don't. They say it is too stressful to adjust to a new baby while you have family there. You want your first few days to be as simi-lar as possible to how they will be on a regular basis. With family and guests staying with you, there can't be consistency. You won't be able to fall into a routine until after everyone leaves. Have them stay in a hotel or with friends, but not with you.

If you have decided to brave it out and have family stay with you, you may have to choose *which* family. This is a battle for you and your wife. There is no right or wrong answer, but you should consider if one family is higher maintenance than another is or if one family would be greatly offended if the other side were to stay at the house.

Do I *Look* Like a Freaking Tour Guide?

If you have guests and family visit-ing from out of town or staying with you, realize that you are not a host, tour guide, or master of ceremonies whose function is to take care of them and entertain them. You have enough on your plate.

The same goes for your wife as well. She should not be exerting any effort other than what it takes to care for herself and the baby. Everyone else comes second and can fend for, feed, clean, and entertain themselves.

This sounds harsh, but even in the best of circumstances, getting used to a new baby in the house and recovering from birth is a trying and tiring experience for everyone involved.

If you have family or guests staying with you, they should not expect to be entertained and waited on, as they might be if this were a regular visit. Anyone who stays with you or comes over should expect to help and contribute to making life easier for mom, baby, and you. This goes for in-laws, parents, siblings, coworkers, and everyone else except for the UPS guy.

The Nights Are the Roughest

Unanimously, veteran daddies agree that the most difficult aspect of being a new parent is caring for a baby throughout the night. Your child will disrupt your sleep patterns, have you scratching your head, and at times push you and your wife to the verge of tears, thinking that you are the worst parents in the world. If you are lucky, your baby may develop a sleep schedule quickly. Accomplishing this takes a mix of practice and the cooperation of your baby, which can't be taken for granted. It is more common for babies not to be on a schedule until they are several months old.

The Crying Never Seems to End

The commercials and media only show the cute, sweet, laughing babies, and when they do show a baby who is upset or crying, we only have to endure it for a few moments. We also have the luxury of changing the channel.

While your baby may be cute and sweet, I guarantee that she will be upset and inconsolable for periods of longer than five minutes. This can happen at any time and for a variety of reasons, some of which are completely beyond your control. Fortunately, you can do something about most of the reasons your child is crying.

It sounds extremely basic, but it helps to remember that when your child cries, she is trying to tell you something. It is up to you to be the detective to determine what is making her cry. You will ultimately develop a mental checklist that you run down every time you hear your baby cry. The main reasons include a dirty or wet diaper—you would cry too, if you had to sit in that stuff—hunger, or gas. As your child grows older, her cries may mean different things, such as she wants to play, but young babies' needs are pretty simple. This, however, doesn't stop you and your wife from feeling like the worst parents in the world when you can't console your child. Eventually, you will get the hang of it.

You Aren't a Bad Parent

Take turns when possible. If you're up at three in the morning trying to care for a newborn who has been crying for ninety minutes straight, sleep is not the only thing that you are short on. Your patience, and your wife's, may be running out as well. If possible, take turns. If you are growing more and more frustrated, the baby can sense it and you won't be able to calm her down.

Crying is something that you will have to get used to. Babies will cry whether you like it or not. It is healthy and normal and is not an indication that you are doing something wrong. You are not a bad parent. You are just a rookie. You have not done this before and are not expected to calm a child like a hospital nurse. You have to develop your parenting skills and adjust to your child. Every child is different in what he likes, dislikes, and what will calm him.

You Do Not Have a Bad Baby

You can be pushed to the brink and start to think irrationally when you are sleep-deprived. Some parents question their competence as parents, while a few will even question if something is wrong with their child.

Byron, a professor in Chicago, says he thought his baby had developed colic, that is, uncontrollable crying in a healthy child. "My wife and I couldn't do anything to calm our daughter. She started shortly after we brought her home. She would cry for hours. We would try to feed her, rock her, play music, change her diapers. Nothing seemed to work. My wife became so distraught that she seriously asked me if we just got a bad baby. For a few days, she even started to pull back from the baby. We took our daughter back to the doctor and he discovered that she wasn't getting enough to eat.

My wife had been breast feeding, but wasn't producing enough milk, so as a result, my daughter was starving. She would feed for what seemed like a long time; she just wasn't getting anything. Once we discovered this and supplemented my daughter's feedings with formula, she was fine."

Colic

About 20 percent of all babies develop colic. Colic is a general term used to describe uncontrollable crying of any type. The crying must be consistent and last for several hours every day. No one knows exactly what causes it, but experts believe that colic is caused by gas or indigestion. Some people think it is related to the mother's diet.

If your child has colic, try to be patient and don't worry. The baby is uncomfortable but will not be harmed or suffer any long-term effects. Colic can last several weeks up to nine months. Ways to help your child include rocking, applying gentle pressure on the child's tummy to relieve gas, and swinging. Some people even take their baby for a ride in the car or place them on the washing machine or dryer. The motion relieves them.

Regardless of the challenges you face, it will get better, and above all, it is worth it.

THE FIRST FEW DAYS

- Your wife may still not be very mobile and may still be experiencing bleeding, particularly if she required stitches. If she had a C-section, she might even be in bed.
- For the first day or two, try to limit the number of visitors and activities around your house. Block out a few uninterrupted hours for your new family to be home alone.
- Establish set visiting hours.
- Give your wife plenty of time to take naps, clean up, and feed the baby. And don't be afraid to reschedule visits if your wife or the baby aren't feeling well.
- Have relatives stay in a hotel or with friends, but not with you.
- If you have family or guests staying with you, they should not expect to be entertained and waited on, as they might be if this were a regular visit.
- When your child cries, she is trying to tell you something. The top reasons include a dirty or wet diaper, hunger, or gas.
- Babies will cry whether you like it or not. It is healthy and normal and is not an indication that you are doing something wrong. You are not a bad parent. You are just a rookie.

27

Can I Have My Wife Back Now?

Even after the birth of a child, many men still find themselves saying, "C'mon, you mean that forty weeks of this isn't enough? I want my wife back now." Just because your wife has had the baby certainly doesn't mean that your wife, or your life, will return to normal. This is not like having bad indigestion and feeling better an hour after taking Tums.

That She-Devil Is Back

The hormone cocktail that you may have had the pleasure of enduring several months earlier as your wife explored the world of multiple personalities is back. Now that the child is born, your wife's hormone levels and internal chemistry are returning to prepregnancy levels, but they can still cause havoc with her emotions and moods until they find a perfect balance. She may be moody, weepy, and irritable.

Some of these mood swings can be attributed to hormones. Other experts claim that women suffer a natural emotional letdown after the child arrives because they have been riding such a euphoric high during pregnancy and birth. While those are two solid reasons that can explain your wife's behavior, sometimes it is simply due to the fact that she is completely exhausted and overwhelmed.

This Isn't as Easy as It Looks

Some guys think that women are instinctively good mothers, but every woman is different. Parenting does not always come naturally or easily to everyone. Calming and caring for a newborn is overwhelming, particularly if you have no experience. It is even more difficult if you have a high-need child or a baby with colic.

Even if your wife is handling the child superbly, her physical workload is taxing and can't be sustained for long. Since the birth of your child, your wife has slept for maybe only three or four hours at a time. When she has been awake, she has likely had a child firmly attached to her breast for about an hour each feeding.

And that is assuming that she can easily feed the child without his biting her nipple until it is raw.

Once the child has finished feeding and has been burped and changed, about two hours have passed. Your wife then will try to put the child back to bed, which can take another thirty minutes or so. When your wife finally is able to put the child down, dry her nipples, and care for herself after the feeding—maybe use the bathroom or grab something to eat— she may have an hour to herself before the baby is up and the cycle starts again. This cycle can be overwhelming, so much so that some rookie mommies said that they have gone days without getting dressed or taking care of themselves. After a few days of this, your wife will be ready to either go on vacation or be committed.

These ups and downs are actually pretty common. At least 50 to 80 percent of rookie mothers experience moodiness, which is often referred to as the baby blues, a mild form of depression. It can start a few days after the baby is born and can last for up to two or three weeks. Pretty soon the fog will lift and your wife will start to get a handle on her new role as mother, wife, and superwoman. With your help, support, and patience, she will snap out of this in a few weeks.

Postpartum Depression

However, if this behavior persists for longer than two or three weeks, or if your wife starts to have over-

whelming feelings that she can't take care of her child, loss of appetite, panic attacks, or irrational fears that she will harm her child, then she may be suffering from postpartum depression. This affects up to 30 percent of all women who give birth. This condition can last for sometimes up to a year. It does not mean that your wife is a bad mother or that you have failed to be there or provide as a husband.

If your wife suffers from postpartum depression, which can be diagnosed by her doctor, you can help her by being supportive, listening to her, helping with the baby when possible, and helping her to relax around the house. Her stress about caring for the child, money, work, or the condition of the house may be contributing factors. Let her know that she doesn't have to be perfect. You might offer to take the baby for several hours a day so she can get out of the house, maybe go to the movies with a friend. You might even get her a certificate for a spa or salon. In time it should pass, but if not, you should consult your pediatrician.

She Doesn't Have to Be Perfect

In addition to the stress of caring for a child and the natural changes going on inside her body, your wife is concerned about the changes to the outside of her body as well. If she is not back to her prepregnancy weight and fitting into her prepregnancy jeans within a month, she will be upset. She will start to compare herself to her friends, to old pictures of herself, and even to Cindy Crawford. I promise that you will hear your wife say, "Look at her. She looks great. There is no *way* she had a baby. I hate her." Don't rush your wife to go on any diets or to lose the weight quickly, especially if she is nursing. You can support her and help her to lose weight by offering to put the baby in the stroller and taking a family walk.

Sitting around all day in gowns and leaky nursing bras would make anyone depressed. She will likely be having some self-esteem issues about her weight and looks, so positively reinforce her ego and give her an opportunity to look beautiful. Take her out to dinner or to a show. Give her a chance to dress up and feel pretty.

Okay, When Can We Have Sex?

Unless you are part of the .0001 percent of couples that had a wild, raging sex life all throughout pregnancy and right up until the moment you took your wife to the hospital, chances are now that it has been several weeks since the baby was born, you are, shall we say … extremely horny.

Even if you had a moderate amount of sex during pregnancy, since the birth of your child it has still been at least several weeks since you and your wife have been intimate. The question on the minds of most guys after the baby arrives is, "When can we have sex?" Sure, your wife may love you and want to be close to you, but the actual thought of sex

shortly after giving birth frankly never enters her mind for the obvious reason that she may have required stitches to repair her torn or cut vagina.

Gynecologists suggest that couples can resume sex approximately six weeks after a woman gives birth. While it is technically possible to have sex sooner than that, experts don't recommend it. Probably neither will your wife. Even after six weeks your wife may not feel frisky enough or even physically or emotionally up for making love. You can't push it. She has been through a lot. Until she is ready, keep up the cold showers and the Victoria's Secret catalogs that you are so well acquainted with.

Why Is It So Tough for Her to Get Back in the Swing of Things?

Even six weeks or longer after giving birth, your wife may still be sensitive in her genital area. Quite frankly, sex may be uncomfortable or even painful for her for a little while after you resume having sex. She knows this and is probably not looking forward to the prospect of pain. It has nothing to do with you. When you do resume sex, realize that initially she may not be able to produce as much lubricant as before. Veteran daddies suggest a little KY jelly in this situation.

Another reason she may be reluctant to jump back in bed is because she is self-conscious about her body. Women lose their pregnancy weight differently. Some women are within five pounds of their prepregnancy weight within a few weeks. (Your wife will automatically hate these women.) Others may retain some of their pregnancy weight for as long as a year or may never get rid of it all.

Pregnancy can change a woman's body forever, but this doesn't mean that she is going to be overweight. If it is still only a few weeks after she has given birth and her body is still full, she may be uncomfortable with her body or not feel sexy. She may be nervous about being naked in front of you. Reassure her that you find her attractive, and do not comment about any changes or differences that you notice. This especially goes for her breasts.

If she is breast-feeding, her breasts will be larger than previously. This is a plus for you. Unfortunately, they are also fully functional, meaning that not only might they be sensitive, they may also leak milk when touched or aroused. Regardless of how you feel about this—excited, indifferent, or repulsed—don't say anything or draw any undue attention to her body.

Can We Just Take a Nap Instead?

Finally, no matter how much you both want to have sex, when it comes down to it you may want to take a nap more than you want to take a romp. Couples claim that in the first year of being parents, fatigue contributed more to altering their sex habits than anything else.

How Important Is Contraception?

Very, unless you want to go through this whole experience again in nine months. When you finally do have sex, make sure that you use a condom. A common old wives' tale says that a woman cannot get pregnant while she is nursing. Wrong. Wrong. Wrong. How do you think couples have children within a year of each other? If your wife is nursing, she will not be able to take birth control pills as long as your child is drinking breast milk. So that means contraception is up to you. You will soon find out how wonderful kids are, but get some mileage on your new baby before you go back for seconds. Don't take chances.

It's Been Awhile

It may have been several months since the two of you have been with each other. And a lot of changes have taken place since then. Both of you may wonder if it will be the same. It is not uncommon for couples to be nervous the first time they make love after having a baby. Don't put any pressure on yourselves or make a big deal if you don't rock the rafters. Just relax and have fun. Make each other comfortable.

One great way to get back in the swing of things is to plan to go on a first date after the baby is born, preferably about six weeks after the birth. Hire a baby-sitter or ask grandma and grandpa to stay with your baby. You can go for a romantic evening out or you can even plan to spend the night away from home at a hotel. Chris, a veteran dad in Memphis, made plans for his in-laws to watch his newborn son for a Friday night shortly after he was born. He made reservations at a romantic hotel in town and took his wife out for dinner and an adult evening away from baby.

You may think that you can't leave the baby overnight. Don't worry, you are not bad parents if you do. The truth is that your wife may be ready for a break. Work on getting your relationship back on track. Remember, part of being a good parent is being a good partner.

DADDY SMARTS TOP TIPS on GETTING YOUR WIFE BACK

- Now that the child is born, your wife's hormone levels and internal chemistry are returning to pre-pregnancy levels, but they can still cause havoc with her emotions and moods until they find a perfect balance.
- At least 50 to 80 percent of rookie mothers experience moodiness, often referred to as the baby blues, a mild form of depression. With your help, support, and patience, she will snap out of this in a few weeks.

- Postpartum depression—including overwhelming feelings that she can't take care of her child, loss of appetite, panic attacks, or irrational fears that she will harm her child—affects up to 30 percent of all women who give birth.
- Positively reinforce her ego and give her an opportunity to look beautiful.
- Even after six weeks, sex may be uncomfortable or even painful for her.
- She may be nervous about being naked in front of you. Reassure her that you find her attractive, and do not comment about any changes or differences that you notice.
- Unless you want to go through this whole experience again in nine months, use contraception.
- Plan a first date after the baby is born, preferably about six weeks after the birth.

Diaper Do's and Don'ts When changing your baby, boys and girls are a little different. With girls your primary objective is to avoid any poop coming in contact with the vagina. It is important for you to wipe in a downward motion, away from the vagina.

With little boys, your primary objective is to avoid being peed on. You can wipe them down or up. However, it is highly recommended that you place a baby wipe or wash-cloth over your son's penis the moment the diaper is removed. It should remain there until the last possible moment. Your kid will be able to shoot a three-foot arc behind his head that would rival anything at Yellowstone.

When changing a boy in the beginning, you also need to be aware of and care for his penis if he was recently circumcised. For the first few days, you will need to pull back the skin every time you change him and wipe away any blood. Doctors recommend that you pull back the foreskin every time you change him for about a year to avoid it reattaching.

Diapers are easy to change once you get the hang of it. Disposable diapers have a picture in the front and adhesive tabs, so all you really need to do is place your child on his back, lift his feet and bottom in the air to place the diaper beneath him, pull the diaper up over his genital area, and use the tape to attach the back to the front. Make sure that it fits snugly or you can have what we like to call in the Richardson casa a "blow out."

28

Baby Basics

You have looked everywhere. You have checked the car, looked in the diaper bag, and called the hospital and you still can't find directions for this thing. You can't even find the receipt.

Taking care of a baby can be intimidating, but with a little practice and quick study, you will be handling your offspring like a veteran in no time.

It's Like Holding a Football ... Just Don't Spike It

There are several ways to hold a baby. You can keep him close to your chest, with his head on your shoulder or chest. You can cradle him with his head in the crook of your arm and with you supporting his back and bottom with your hand. There is also the famous "football" hold. It is very helpful if your baby is gassy. Place the baby, stomach down, on your forearm so that his head is in your hand and his butt is near the crook of your arm. His arms and legs can dangle. It can relieve pressure on his stomach.

How to Cure a Gassy Baby: The "Rose Hold"

There is another hold that my wife and I owe our sanity to. We simply call it the "Rose hold," named in honor of a wise baby-sitter who showed it to us. Our daughter Samantha had colic and was frequently gassy. We couldn't find a suitable hold for her. She would cry and cry until one day when Rose came to sit for us, she took Sam and held her. Sam's back was pressed against Rose's stomach, and Rose had placed her arm around the lower part of the baby's stomach. Much like a waiter holds a towel on his arm. Samantha gave out the loudest belch of her young life and was happy as can be. We could hold her for hours like that.

Find what works for you, but regardless, make sure that you support the baby's head. Their little necks aren't yet developed and won't be able to support their big melon heads for several months.

Picking Up Your Baby

The best way is to reach underneath the baby's back and bottom at the same time. Make sure that you cradle or support her neck while you are doing this. Head and neck support are critical. You can also pick up the child underneath her arms. Never ever pick up an infant by the arms or limbs.

Feed Me, Seymour

If your wife breast-feeds, you won't have to worry about this for several weeks until she begins pumping breast milk to use in bottles. Breast milk can be refrigerated but must be used shortly after it is pumped unless it is frozen for later use.

Bottle types and styles vary but the rules are generally the same. If heating a bottle, do not use a microwave. It can alter the milk or formula. Use a hot water tap or boiling water. There are also special bottle heaters you can buy. Keep one in your bathroom or bedroom for the first few weeks so you don't have to go to the kitchen every time.

Babies don't eat much early on. You may fill a bottle with only two ounces, and that may be enough to fill your baby. You don't have to fill a bottle to the rim.

Test the bottle temperature on your own skin before giving it to your child to make sure it isn't too hot. Squirt a drop or two on the inside of your wrist.

A nipple must be sterilized before it is used for the first time and after each time the child uses it. Rinsing it off will not do. You must put it in the dishwasher or use scalding hot water.

Much like a glass of milk, a bottle can't sit out for a long time and be reused. It can become tainted and harmful to your child. Get a fresh bottle every time. Do not reuse formula or milk. If you are traveling or keeping a bottle in your diaper bag, unless it is powdered formula, use an ice pack or something else that can act as a cooler so the formula or milk doesn't spoil.

There really is no better bonding experience than feeding your baby. In the beginning, sit down to feed your child. With practice, you will be able to walk around and talk on a cell phone while feeding your baby, but let's walk before we run. Sit in a comfortable upright chair and place the baby in the crook of your arm. Her head should be elevated. Do not shove the bottle into her mouth or force it in any way. She won't use her hands to shove it away or pull it near in the beginning. You have to read her signals. Gently rub the bottle nipple on her lips and apply pressure to put it in her mouth. If she is hungry, she will take the bottle. You can put it a little farther in her mouth at that point. If she is not hungry or is having a difficult time latching on to the bottle, she will purse her lips or attempt to spit it out. Try for a different angle that may be easier for her. If this continues, then wait a little bit. She may not be hungry right then.

Baby CPR

If you should ever discover that your baby has stopped breathing, whether from SIDS or another ca you may be able to save her using cardiopulmonary resuscitation (C

I hope that such an emergency never arises, but in the event that does, call 911. You can also have peace of mind for you and your and anyone else who cares for yo child by taking a baby CPR class. to your pediatrician, hospital, or local Red Cross to learn about cla Baby CPR is a little different from adult CPR, mostly because your patient is so much smaller. It is a investment.

www.poop.com

So, you want the poop on poo Here goes. For the first few days, baby's poops will be a thick gooey like substance called meconium. Inside the womb, your baby swal lowed amniotic fluid and anythin else that happened to be in there These first few poops get all that of his system. Meconium is about tough to remove from your kid's as it is to remove tar from your c

This will last a few days to a w Then things will become more so Sorry to be graphic, but they will be solid like a log but more like a patty. You will be happy to know baby poops don't really smell. Yo can relax. Your kid's diapers won reek until he or she starts eating food.

This is when poop or other matter oozes out the sides or over the top of the diaper. It's your basic containment problem.

Wash Your Hands

Babies' immune systems are still not fully developed, so be religious about washing your hands, especially after changing your child. There are many antibacterial soaps and even gels and lotions that you can use in case you aren't near a sink. Keep a few scattered around the house, in the car, and in your dad bag.

If you are going to allow other people to hold the baby, gently remind them that the soap and towels are by the sink in the kitchen. Everyone, including you, should wash their hands before holding or playing with the baby. It is perfectly fine for you to ask someone to honor this request.

How Can I Have a Calm and Smart Baby?

Music calms the savage beast. It also calms your little savage as well. Recent studies have found that classical music, including Mozart and Brahms, may help develop babies' brains and improve their math and language ability. Some hospitals are even giving classical music CDs to families as they leave the hospital. I look at it as a safe bet. If it works, great. If it doesn't work, at least it helps put my kids to sleep.

DADDY SMARTS TOP TIPS on **BABY BASICS**

- **When holding your baby, support his head.**
- **To pick up your baby, reach underneath the baby's back and bottom at the same time. Never ever pick up an infant by the arms or limbs.**
- **When heating a bottle, do not use a microwave. It can alter the milk or formula. Use a hot water tap or boiling water.**
- **Test the bottle temperature on your own skin before giving it to your child to make sure it isn't too hot. Squirt a drop or two on the inside of your wrist.**
- **Nipples must be sterilized before they are used for the first time and after each use.**
- **Bottles can't sit out for a long time and then be reused. They can become tainted and harmful to your child. Get a fresh bottle every time.**
- **When putting your baby down to sleep always place him on his back. Do not place him on his tummy, facedown.**
- **Be religious about washing your hands, especially after changing your child.**

29

Flying Solo: First Time Alone with Baby

After being cooped up in the house for a couple of weeks, your wife will finally be feeling well enough and skinny enough to venture back out into public. However, considering that she has most likely spent the past few weeks with a five-to-twelve-pound appendage hanging from her boobs every three hours, she might want a few moments of personal time, even if it is as simple as going to a store.

This is not an opportunity for you to call the baby-sitter or your mother-in-law. You are going to have to learn how to care for your child by yourself sooner or later. Why not now?

Many rookie dads are terrified of this moment. You may be shell-shocked from the nighttime crying. You may not know what to do without the backup of your wife. You may be fearful that if he cries, you won't be able to get him to stop, or you may even be scared of inadvertently harming the child. But you are better than you think. Now is the time to prove it to yourself and to your wife.

Start Small

The best way to start is small. Your first time alone should only be two or three hours. This way you can build up to more and you won't get overwhelmed. If you feel that you can take it, call your wife and tell her to stay out longer because you are teaching your little genius how to re-finance the mortgage.

Speaking of being prepared, have all of your tools, diapers, wipes, changes of clothes, burp cloths, and bottles ready. When your baby wakes up, you will be ready to take great care of her and won't fumble around trying to find stuff. The worst thing would be to call your wife saying, "Honey, do you know where the wipes are?"

Keep the baby monitor nearby and listen for her to wake up. Go in from time to time and check on her. Stay in the house. Don't go outside and do yard work, work on the car, or exercise. Try not to get involved in something that you can't leave in the middle. You need to be prepared if your child needs you.

Remember the Moment

Veteran daddies all say that this is a special moment that they remember, even though not much may happen. It is a rite of passage. Document it. Take pictures. One veteran daddy set up a video camera on a tripod and filmed himself taking care of his son. He held the boy up to the camera and explained what was going on. He sang songs to the baby and filmed his feeding the boy as well. It was a great way to capture some special time together.

Stepping Out with My Baby

Now that you have proven you can handle being alone with your baby, you are ready to move on to the next step. Today is graduation day.

Let your wife know ahead of time that you would like to take the baby on an outing. She be laugh her butt off and wonder how you will cope, but you will show her.

Once you have ventured out with the baby, you are officially a veteran daddy, capable of handling anything … at least until your child is three months old. But that is another book.

Start small. For your first time out with the baby alone, you don't want to plan an airplane trip across five states. Let's start small, like maybe to Starbucks or the bagel shop.

Plan an activity of probably no longer than a couple of hours at the most. You can always build up to a longer trip. You have a lifetime together.

Where Do I Change My Baby?

Guys are highly creative where this is concerned. Essentially, we have no shame. If my kids knew half of the places I've changed them and exposed their bare bottoms they would die of embarrassment. So would my wife for that matter.

Many men's rooms are fitted for changing stations, These are built into the wall and fold down so you can lay your child on it. Just take junior in the rest room with you. If they do not have one, it can be tricky. Balance is the key. It is better to change your child's smelly bum in the back of your car than to risk dropping him. If you drive an SUV, it works out really well. You can pop the back and change away. Your kid can get a little sun on his cheeks too.

You want to be aware of other people, however. It is common sense, but as the saying goes, "If common sense were so common, more people would have it." Don't change your child in a restaurant, in a store, or anywhere near food. Promptly remove the soiled item and wash your hands.

She Fell Asleep in the Car

Many babies love riding in the car. The motion puts them to sleep almost immediately. Make sure that you keep the sun out of her eyes. You can buy special car shades or film to reduce the glare. Also make sure that she gets plenty of air without having it blow directly on her.

I've Taken Less Gear on Vacation

Be prepared to take a travel steamer. At least, it will seem like you should. You will need your car seat, a stroller or baby carrier, and of course you will need your daddy bag.

Remember, I said to get a cool, manly diaper bag and not some foo-foo purse. If you carry a cool bag, the rest doesn't matter, until your kid screams or poops. For that event, you should carry about four extra diapers, wipes (which come in convenient travel sizes), an extra change of clothes, and one full bottle and a spare. Nipples can break or you may not be able to wash the first bottle out. Veteran dads keep a spare diaper in their car, stuff a bottle in their pocket and can improvise with anything else. Veteran daddies are kind of like McGuyver, the TV hero who was a poor man's James Bond. The guy could build a laser out of a pencil, a paper clip, and chewing gum.

Traveling with a Baby

Once you have mastered this, you may want to hit the road and visit grandma or grandpa. Let me give a few words to the wise regarding road trips. Travel during your child's nap time so she isn't as squirmy and uncomfortable. Never feed a baby while a car is moving. Feed the child a lot *before* you start out. You want her fat, happy, and sleepy. Keep plenty of supplies with you in the car. You don't want to be at a Stuckey's in Rear Axle, Idaho, without any formula.

Can't We Just Check the Baby with the Bags?

Airplanes are a different story. Before I had kids, I was the type that never understood why a parent couldn't simply keep his kid quiet on an airplane. Folks, it's easier catching a greased pig than keeping a child quiet on an airplane. On most airlines, kids under two fly free, but that means that if the plane is full, your child sits on your lap.

Many airlines do not allow you to take certain types of car seats on planes. To make things easier on yourself, travel at off-peak hours, when the business crowd is not likely to fly. Take advantage of preboarding services and ask the flight attendant to help you. Don't be a martyr. And finally, when you take off and land, be sure to place a bottle or pacifier in your child's mouth. Babies don't know how to release the pressure in their ears like we do, which is the main reason little babies cry on airplanes. Feeding them does it naturally.

Take a Picture

Have your wife snap a few pictures of you and your child as you venture out into the world alone for the first time. You will treasure these later.

Proud Papa Keeps on Rolling

I had my first outing with my daughter when she was around a month old. I had been waiting almost

frequently asked questions about,
0–95
getting good service at, 132–138,
155–158
labor and. *See* Labor day
nurses at. *See* Nurse(s)
paperwork at, 161–162
routes to, 128
security at, 91–92
taking supplies and equipment from,
159–160
visitors and, 157–158

Induced labor, 129–130
In-laws. *See* Parent(s), of couple having
baby
Iron John, 47

Job(s)
expectant mother's, 27, 59
father's
new baby and, 69–70, 168
taking leave from, 70
taking time off from, 168
Jogger stroller, 76–77

Kung Fu, 51

Labor day
checklist for, 128
driving to hospital and, 128
epidural and, 136–137, 141
expectant mother's needs during,
139–142
false alarms and, 130–131
getting call and, 130
getting ready for, 125–131
night before, 129–130

waiting and, 141
Lamaze, 92–95, 140
Lanugo, 87, 145
Linea nigra, 83
Love
for child, 68
Lovemaking
after childbirth, 52–53, 176–178
anxiety and, 12–13
contraception and, 177
during pregnancy, 49–52
frequency of, 14–15
kinds of, 10–11
positions used in, 11–12, 51–52
to become pregnant, 10–15, 49

Magnum PI, 105
The Man Who Shot Liberty Valance, 104
Mickelson, Amy, 70
Mickelson, Phil, 70
Mother(s)
after childbirth
first night and, 152
gift for, 150–152
placenta and, 147
expectant
breasts and, 82, 83
driving to hospital by, 128
effects of pregnancy upon, 37–43,
81–85
father-to-be's interaction with,
37–43
"glow" and, 82
hormones and, 82
labor and. *See* Labor day
lovemaking and, 49–52
needs of, during labor, 139–142
other, noticing, 67
pregnancy's effects on, 37–43
salary of, budgeting without, 27, 59
See also Pregnancy

Mother(s) *(continued)*
new
breasts and, 53–54, 174–175
hormones and, 174
learning by, 169–170, 174–175
lovemaking and, 52–53
pain and, 167–168
postpartum depression and, 175
working by, staying at home versus,
111–112
Mozart, Wolfgang Amadeus, 183
Music
classical, babies and, 183
in labor and delivery rooms, 126

Name for baby, choosing, 104–109, 150
Nanny
checking up on, 121
child care provided by, 116, 120–121,
122, 168–169
temporary, caring for newborn and,
168–169
testing, 122
National SIDS Alliance, 181
The New American Dictionary of Baby Names,
108
Night nurse, 168–169
Nine Months, 29, 33
Nurse(s)
APGAR test and, 145–146
being nice to, 133, 155–156
getting personal with, 133–134
night, 168–169
problems with, 135–136
Nursery, preparing for baby, 72–73, 127,
161

Obstetrician/gynecologist (OB/GYN)
hospital preferred by, 90
problems with, 135
visits to, with wife, 32–36, 57, 60

Pager, getting ready for labor day and,
127–128
Parent(s)
of couple having baby
as role models, 64–66
help with care of newborn and,
169–170
holding newborn and, 149–150
informing about becoming pregnant, 19–20
informing about labor, 128
learning by, 174–175
unsolicited advice from, dealing
with, 45, 46–47
new
death of, care of child and, 114
lifestyle changes and, 114–115
Paternity leave, 70
Pets, 74
Photos, 147, 162
Picture taking, 147, 162, 185, 186
Placenta, 147
Planet of the Apes, 105
Postpartum depression, 175
Pregnancy
announcement of, 19–21
body growth during, 81–82
doctor's confirmation and, 32
effects of, upon mother-to-be, 37–43,
81–85
expectant father's learning about,
58–59
expectant father's role during, 37–43,
55–63
lovemaking during, 49–52
testing for, at home, 16–18, 32
trimester(s) of
first, 81–82, 86–87
second, 82–83, 87
third, 83–84, 87–88
weight gain during, 61–62, 83,
175–176

Congratulations and good luck with your new family.

I hope that you've enjoyed *Daddy Smarts: A Guide for Rookie Fathers.*

I encourage you to share your stories, tips, comments, and pictures with us and to look for more advice, products, tips, and upcoming books for fathers on our official Web site:

www.daddysmarts.com
Bradley Richardson
Daddy Smarts™
P.O. Box 701420
Dallas, TX 75370
877-DADSMARTS
877-323-7627
Bradley@DaddySmarts.com